FAITH

LIKE A CHILD

FAITH
LIKE A CHILD

DISCOVER *the* SIMPLE JOY
of LOVING GOD

JOHNNY PARKER
WITH JAN PETERSON

Fleming H. Revell
A Division of Baker Book House Co
Grand Rapids, Michigan 49516

© 2003 by Johnny Parker

Published by Fleming H. Revell
a division of Baker Book House Company
P.O. Box 6287, Grand Rapids, MI 49516-6287
www.bakerbooks.com

Printed in the United States of America

Library of Congress Cataloging-in-Publication Data
Parker, Johnny.
    Faith like a child : discover the simple joy of loving God / Johnny
Parker with Jan Peterson.
        p.   cm.
    ISBN 0-8007-5858-7 (pbk.)
    1. Faith. 2. God—Love. 3. Christian life. 4. Parent and child—Religious aspects—Christianity. I. Peterson, Jan. II. Title.
BV4637.P36 2003
242—dc21   2003010532

To my sons, the three Js—Johnny, Jordan, and Joel. I realize I'll never graduate from the University of Fatherhood. During the course of watching you grow and studying your lives, I have been greatly affected. I feel as though I've been experiencing a graduate-level intimacy with God and in my relationships as a result of your lives. Your daily stories have caused my heart to come alive to God in an incredible way and to experience him as my daddy.

To the memory of Erika Georgette Smith, whose story has taught many that life is a gift and not an entitlement. You are now enjoying heaven's playgrounds. We miss you and we love you.

CONTENTS

Living Authentic Lives

Forgiveness

Walking in Faith

Obedience

God's Mercy and Grace

Who Jesus Is

Our Speech

CONTENTS

ACKNOWLEDGMENTS

This book has been birthed as a result of the help of several family members, friends, and professional associates. Thanks for making it a reality:

Lezlyn (Peaches) for encouraging me and helping me process the different stories. You are my lady!

Johnny and Gwendolyn Parker and Kent and Doreen Miller for your selfless giving as parents and grandparents. You amaze me!

In memory of my grandparents, Charles and Rosa Lee Walker, who modeled an authentic commitment to God and introduced me to his love as a child. I look forward to seeing you on the other side and once again experiencing your biscuits.

My agent, Bruce Barbour, and Vicki Crumpton at Revell, who believed in me and in this project.

Phyllis Herman for providing first-class transcribing of my tapes at the eleventh hour. Once again, you prove to be incredible.

Eugene Seals for working your magic in critiquing and editing some of the stories. You da' man!

Mitzie, Dex, Denzel, Zanise, Janelle, and Taylor for all your love and support.

Bill and Franky Wright for your friendship and your professional assistance.

Aaron and Miranda Robertson for the way you dote on my sons and love them as if they were your own.

Pastor John K. Jenkins Sr. and the staff and members of First Baptist Church of Glenarden for embracing me and allowing me the privilege to serve.

All my uncles, aunts, and cousins—Parkers, Walkers, Campbells, Corbetts, and Baileys—with whom I share a rich heritage.

Marty Grainger, Joel Freeman, Crawford Loritts, Dave Jones, Clarence Shuler, Rod Cooper, Pat Morley, Rich Hurst, and Tom Fortson for being my mentors and modeling authentic manhood.

Clarence and Pat Parker for opening up your home and hearts to a young, struggling college student over twenty years ago. Thank you for your friendship.

Family Life Ministries and Man in the Mirror for allowing me to be a part of a dream team and to experience a wonderful adventure in serving.

Adrienne Mercer, Rev. William Berkeley, and others for allowing me to tell some of their childhood stories.

Pastors David Anderson, Marshall Awesberry, Kenneth Barney, Keith Battle, Michael Black, Irv Clark, Ronald Crawford, Michael Easley, Bernard Fuller, James Hall, Clifford Johnson, Jerry Martin, Stan Ponz, Thomas Rich, Mark Saunders, Greg Sims, Lon Solomon, Terry Streeter, and Jonathan Weaver for the privilege of sharing these stories at your churches.

Special thanks to Jan Peterson, who enthusiastically and selflessly gave to this project. You were the hub. You're a magical writer, and your spirit is infectious. I so enjoy working with you, and we do make a great team!

INTRODUCTION

For much of my life, I've struggled with trusting God and being convinced that he *really* loves me. The truth is that I secretly resented those people who spoke with assurance of intimacy with God and his love for them. Why didn't I have this intimate loving relationship? The reality of this question was forever answered when I became a father. I was prompted to write this book as a result of observing my sons and realizing the parallels between their behavior and relationship with me and my behavior and relationship with God. The joys, temptations, and struggles they have are similar to the ones I have, but on a different level. The way they wrestle to live from my perspective and to follow my instructions is much the same way I grapple with trusting God and following his loving plans for my life. Aha! No wonder Jesus placed a high premium on children and viewing life through the lens of their world. Listen to Jesus' words, "Whoever becomes simple and elemental again, like this child, will rank high in God's kingdom. What's more, when you receive the childlike on my account, it's the same as receiving me" (Matt. 18:4–5 MESSAGE).

In one of the stories, "God's Needles," I describe how kids detest receiving shots. They cry, they squirm, and they totally resist. Yet from the parents' and doctor's viewpoint, needles are necessary for health purposes. Loving parents cuddle their children and attempt to reassure them during this highly stressful procedure. After the nurse is finished, the child usually receives a treat. Isn't the same thing true for adults? We experience our own version of needles—problems and trials. God allows them and says they are good for our spiritual health and character development. Like a loving parent, God cuddles us and is present during the ordeal. God also offers a treat in the form of blessing, reward, or crown.

Watching my sons has given me a rich and fresh perspective of life and of God. It's as though I've grown from a water-ski level faith to a deep-sea intimacy with God, being reminded of the simple things and the things that matter most.

I have shared these stories as part of counseling, in seminars, in sermons, and at conferences, and I have seen how *the light goes on* for the hearer. Many have commented how the stories enabled them to view life and see God in a refreshing way.

My hope and desire is that you might experience the same.

1

TO BE A KID AGAIN

I read an article written by a young mom who said one of her favorite parts of being a stay-at-home mom was getting to be a child again. She talked about playing dress-up with her girls, building a fort on their pond with her son, and rolling down the grassy hill at their local park so many times that her head was spinning. I laughed as I read her words because I could feel her joy. It was such a pure honesty—that she had rediscovered the child in her through her children and recognized it as a good thing. It left me thinking about my grumpy state of late. How much better if I could find the child in me while I can enjoy it with my children.

It is no accident that Jesus drew a picture for us using the innocence and humility of children. He stressed a child's humility as a pattern for us, saying, "I tell you the truth, unless you change and become like little children, you will never enter the kingdom of heaven. Therefore, whoever humbles himself like this child is the greatest in the kingdom of heaven" (Matt. 18:3–4). Why? They are at square one in their lives, simple and unburdened by all of the stuff we accumulate walking in the world. They trust, love, and live without considering first what's in it for them.

Beyond their humility, children have an innate sense of joy. They know how to keep life simple and how to enjoy their days. I once heard a speaker reference a study that found that the average four-year-old laughs over forty times a day—but the average forty-year-old laughs only about four times a day.

Ecclesiastes says, "There is a time for everything, and a season for every activity under heaven . . . a time to weep and a time to laugh" (Eccl. 3:1, 4). Clearly, God realized that laughter had a place in our lives, whether we are young or old. King David had a wife who could not appreciate laughter and play. Michal saw King David dancing and playing as the ark of the covenant was carried into the City of David, and she despised him in her heart (1 Chron. 15:29). Surely Michal had play and laughter in her soul at one time, but perhaps it had been tamed or shamed out of her. Maybe she was surrounded by adults who said things like, "Wipe that goofy look off your face," "Stop acting silly," "Stop clowning around," "You need to grow up." Does this sound familiar? Perhaps you heard these words as a child—or perhaps you've said them to your children.

As adults, it's important that we don't forget how to laugh and how to play. It is also important that we understand there is a great difference between being *childlike* in spirit and *childish* in spirit. A childish spirit is immature, while a childlike spirit promotes trust and strength. A childish spirit makes a game out of life, while a childlike spirit remembers to find joy on the path.

I love the words of William Arthur Ward. He says, "Laughter and play are the pole that adds balance to our steps as we walk the tightrope of life." Laughter and play serve as our shock absorbers, helping us over the potholes we are guaranteed to speed over along the road of life. I'll never forget walking through a graveyard and seeing a tombstone with these words: "Here lies a beautiful person and here lies next to her a grumpy old grouch." Even in death or loss, this person had a spirit of laughter or levity about him.

Laughter is healthy. It gives us a place where we can recharge our emotional batteries. It gives us a new perspective, and it gives us ways of managing the stresses in our lives.

16

What are you doing today to cultivate a spirit of laughter and play in your home and in your life? Maybe it's as simple as throwing a Frisbee with your son after school, even though you *should* be folding laundry. Maybe it's playing peek-a-boo with a friend's toddler or playing hide-and-seek with your own kids. A friend of mine has a family ritual in which they go around the table and each person has to perform their goofiest talent—which must be different from the talent they shared the time before. It is a hoot, especially when you're the unsuspecting dinner guest!

God worked six days, but on the seventh day he rested, recharged, recreated. Laughter and play is a way for us to rest, recharge, and recreate. Be intentional about finding time for fun and laughter. Go ahead and color outside the lines. Recapture the child in you.

There is a time for everything, and a season for every activity under heaven . . . a time to weep and a time to laugh.

ECCLESIASTES 3:1, 4

2 ———————————————————

ARE WE HAVING
FUN YET?

A few years ago, my wife and I surprised our kids with a trip to one of those fancy amusement parks. Knowing that we had an early drive the next morning, we tucked them into bed a bit early, and once we were sure they were sound asleep, we quickly began packing suitcases for the five of us. Although we were physically drained by the time we dropped into bed that night, we were filled with anticipation for the joy that our boys would experience over the upcoming few days.

We woke the boys up early the next morning, helped them, in their sleepy fog, to get dressed, and headed out the door. It didn't take long for their curiosity to wake up! The thrill of the adventure and fun activities in the van kept them distracted, but once we crossed over the bridge to a neighboring state, the questions were flying. "Daddy, where are we going?" they asked over and over again. I kept a quiet smile on my face, but inside, my heart was bursting at what was to come.

We had an absolutely amazing time on this trip, and as much as I enjoyed experiencing the thrill from the grown-up side of things, this paled in comparison to the great thrill I got from watching my sons laugh and play. Their joy filled my heart. I consider it a great privilege to be able to cultivate experiences of fun and pleasure for my boys. Whether it's taking them to an amusement park, spending a day at the beach, or just letting them have ice cream for breakfast (once in a very great while, of course!), I am blessed by their joy.

So it is with God. In John 10:10, Christ says, "I have come that they may have life, and have it to the full." He is talking about you and me. God *wants* us to have fun while we are on earth. He wants us to find joy in life, and his heart is filled when he sees us laugh, giggle, or glow in a moment of pleasure.

Too often we lose sight of the richness that God desires for our life. We get bogged down in our daily grind, losing sight of the wonderful moments God has planned for us. We focus on tomorrow or we concentrate on the "oops" in our day instead of the "ahh."

I can remember the days when I saw God as the stern taskmaster. I thought the fun times were almost a secret—something I could slip in while God was busy with someone else. God was only concerned with keeping me on the straight and narrow path, right? This certainly couldn't include fun and laughter.

Thinking of this picture makes me almost tremble inside, because it reminds me of the amazing work God can do in each of us. He has taken me from that place and allowed me to see how truly wrong my perspective was. While God is a just God who desires that I live my life for him, he is at the same time a loving, caring Father who wants the best for me. While pain and suffering are part of my life, so, too, are joy, laughter, pleasure, bliss, elation, and delight.

God has our life plan before him, filled with experiences designed to give us joy. Allow yourself the pleasure of enjoying the small moments that fill your day. Remember that just as the joy on your child's face fills your heart with song, your joy fills your Father's heart. He relishes in your laughter and delight. Perhaps these moments are but a small glimpse of the euphoria that awaits us in heaven.

I came so they can have real and eternal life, more and better life than they ever dreamed of.

JOHN 10:10 MESSAGE

3 ————————

NO MORE DIRTY FEET

I recently talked with a good friend who told me of a poignant, powerful childhood experience that marked her young life and most of her adult years. She always perceived her father to love her brothers more than he loved her.

As she recalled, it all seemed to start when she was three, playing in her parents' bedroom on the floor in her bare feet. Her daddy was lying in the bed, and she had this childishly innocent desire to cuddle next to him. When she jumped in bed and cuddled next to her father, he vehemently denied her wishes. He explained, "No, no, no. I do not want to play with you because you have dirty feet, and I might get dirty or catch germs from your dirty feet."

My friend is fifty-five years old now and has been a Christian for some time, but she can look at her relationships with men and see her longing to be accepted and received by men while sometimes having struggles with boundaries. She can trace this back to this vivid scene and the palpable rejection by her father because of her dirty feet.

That is not the end of the story. Recently my friend was visiting with her aged, ill father. She had a special moment with him. He had never told her he loved her, so when the conversation moved in the appropriate direction, she was led to say to him, "Dad, I have always felt that you favored my brothers over me." She told him the story about his devastating rejection of her because of her dirty feet when she was an impressionable three years old. Her father understood her concern and was able to bless her in her adult years and to say to her that he was sorry. He had never known the impact his retort had had on her. He could not even remember it more than fifty years later. He asked her forgiveness, and they held each other and wept.

Life is filled with rejection. Make no mistake—rejection hurts, especially when it comes from the hands of those we count dear and love. We hear over and over in our hearts the voice that rejected us, "You have dirty feet." Its cadence becomes the defining byline.

Perhaps you did not make the cheerleading team or the basketball team. In your heart, you heard a voice saying, "It is because you have dirty feet that you were not good enough." Perhaps someone ended a relationship with you, and you wondered, "Why was I not good enough?" Perhaps in your head you heard the now all-too-familiar refrain, "It is because you have dirty feet." Perhaps you did not make the choir. It is hard not to take this stuff personally. The voice again said, "It is because you have dirty feet."

Perhaps you shared your Christian faith with someone on a plane or at work. When they told you, no, they did not want to pray and they did not want a relationship with Jesus Christ, it was hard not to take it personally. You thought it was because you did not tell it right because of your dirty feet. You might have wondered if maybe you have sinned so terribly, maybe through adultery, maybe through abuse toward someone, or abuse from someone. You wonder, "How can I ever be forgiven—how can I ever be okay?" You think it is impossible.

Maybe you have gone through a divorce after years and years of your spouse's complaining. No matter what the stated criticism, all you heard was, "I have dirty feet. I can never be forgiven. I can never be well. I can never get beyond this because I have dirty feet."

The Bible talks a lot about feet. All of us are born with unholy feet. That is why we are told to take off our shoes when we stand before the burning bush, because the place where we now stand is holy in the face of God.

Jesus came to wash our feet, and he washes our feet when we offer them to him. We may think, "Oh no, Lord. Do not wash me. I am unworthy." But he says to us, "No matter what you have done or not done, only one question needs to be answered: Are you willing to surrender your feet to be washed?"

No matter how dirty, no matter where the feet have been, no matter how dark and unholy, God says, "If you will surrender your feet and lay them before me, I will wash them."

Not only does he want to wash our feet, but he wants to anoint our feet with the ointment of his Spirit as well. He wants to massage our feet with his Spirit so our feet can become like the feet of a deer, which are able to leap and experience new heights and move rapidly in the direction of life in which God wants us to walk and move and have our being.

The Sovereign LORD is my strength; he makes my feet like the feet of a deer, he enables me to go on the heights.

HABAKKUK 3:19

4

SITTING ON GOD'S LAP

I was recently told a story that was shared in a Sunday school class one day. The group was going around the circle sharing a word picture to illustrate how they saw God. One of the women in the group said, "I see God as my father—I just want to crawl into his lap and have him hold me." She went on to share her story:

My heart was silently breaking as my little girl sobbed into my chest. It was one of those gut-wrenching cries that comes from so deep within, the child had to be reminded to breathe. On the parent end of this, I knew that something horrible had happened, but it was only after the calming process that the details came pouring out.

This was the day of the mile run. For some kids, this is no big deal, but for my girl, it was a struggle. Her little body just isn't wired for running at the ripe young age of eight. She loves tennis and she is an amazing swimmer, but of course, these weren't on the list of tasks for second grade P.E. class. It was the day of the mile run.

So my girl had run the mile, only to finish second to last. It wasn't last, she spilled out, but it hurt so badly. As if the actual running wasn't bad enough, the subtle snickers from the other children cemented the pain in my daughter's heart. She felt ridiculed and embarrassed. She felt like a failure—and my heart ached for her.

I heard myself saying that this day would pass. That it wasn't really all that bad. That I knew it hurt desperately, but that in the grand scheme of things, this day would prove not to be important. Five years from now, no one would remember she had finished second to last in the mile run. They might remember the yellow ribbon she got at her swim meet. They would possibly remember her award-winning performance in the elementary spelling bee. They would definitely remember her life-giving smile.

Of course I knew all of these things to be true, and I also knew that nothing I could say would erase the sadness in my daughter's heart. And so we sat . . . and sat . . . and sat. She curled up in my lap, and I tried to hug love into her little soul. We sat. . . .

I don't think I could even begin to count the number of lap moments I have had the privilege of being a part of with my kids. From excited hugs of joy and accomplishment to tender hugs of rebuilding, they are too many to number. I do know that this gift of the lap is one that is in its waning years. My twelve-year-old, besides the fact that he is just plain too big for my lap, needs it less and less frequently—at least in his mind.

And that is the key. We all reach a stage where we just don't need the lap anymore. It becomes uncool, uncomfortable, or just plain weird. Yet, this change is really just a transition phase from crawling into Mommy or Daddy's lap to resting in the lap of our heavenly Father.

Do you see God this way? I remember the day it hit me. I was tired from my trials and desperately wanted a safe place to vent, rest, and be comforted and restored. I actually remember thinking, "I need a lap—too bad I'm way beyond that!" And then I heard God say as clear as day, "Come to me. I will give you rest."

I loved this word picture because it showed the caring, loving side of God. These words illustrated perfectly the way God wants us to come running to him—just as our children come running to us. God understands our weaknesses because Jesus lived in this world.

For we do not have a high priest who is unable to sympathize with our weaknesses, but we have one who has been tempted in every way, just as we are—yet was without sin. Let us then approach the throne of grace with confidence, so that we may receive mercy and find grace to help us in our time of need.

HEBREWS 4:15–16

5

HOLD ME, I'M SCARED

W e've got to let him cry."

"We can't pick him up every night."

"He's got to be able to fall asleep without us always holding, walking, and rocking him."

These were our words to one another nearly every night. Yet we continued to give in to his incessant cry—nearly every night. Seven long months had passed since the birth of our firstborn. As fledgling parents, we had developed some awful habits regarding our son's sleep routine. Our apartment was very small, and the three of us were packed tightly into one bedroom. It gave new meaning to *close fellowship*. We constantly picked him up. Consequently, he refused to sleep unless he was held or could see that we were at least standing nearby.

On the evening of July 4, 1993, Lezlyn and I made a parenting pact. We agreed to set him down at a regular time each night, and if he cried, he cried. This time we meant business. We would only attend to him for wetness or sickness. Otherwise, we would not pick him up, walk him, or rock him. No more "Mr. Nice Guy!"

The first test came—you guessed it—that same night! While 250 million Americans were enjoying fireworks, we were expe-

26

riencing waterworks. John-John awoke crying about 2 A.M., right on schedule. He cried for about thirty minutes! We lay in bed in the dark, looking in his direction but refusing to budge. Physically, he was fine. Yet every fiber within us wanted to rescue him and reassure him that everything was okay. It was tough, but somehow we held our ground (or bed, whichever way you want to look at it). He could not see us, but we could see that he was fine.

He probably wondered, "Why aren't these people coming to check on me and hold me as they've always done? Why aren't they attending to me as much as they did before? I don't like this feeling of being alone." We were nearby. We had not forgotten him or abandoned him, not in a trillion years. But it was crucial for him to learn how to rest and sleep whether or not he could feel our presence.

When I was a child. In the early season of my new birth in Christ, I seemed to experience a double dose of God's presence. I felt his hand with me as I took baby steps in my new spiritual walk. I could sense his Spirit speaking through his Word to my heart. Heaven had come down and glory filled my soul! I felt spiritually warm, cozy, and so connected with my heavenly Father. Then it happened. Just when I was enjoying the spring in my soul, the season changed. The leaves began falling off the trees in my spiritual life. A chill developed around my faith. The pure milk of the Word appeared to be evaporating. What was occurring? Why was God tampering with my springtime? In fact, where was God?

I no longer felt God's presence. Things were not cheery and blooming as they had been in the earlier season. Did God not understand that I had never known any other season? I was not familiar with autumn and winter, and I found them most unpleasant. They were characterized by shorter days and simply not enough light. I missed feeling his presence. I felt doubts and insecurities I had not known before. Was there sin in my life? Did I lose my salvation? Was God upset with me? Where was he? Why did I stop feeling his presence? I wanted my Father back.

Some twenty years later, I've come to realize that was the first of many autumns and winters in my spiritual journey. The psalmist David also encountered wintry seasons in his life. During a period of loneliness and depression, he wrote, "Return, O LORD, rescue my soul; save me because of Your loving kindness. . . . I am weary with my sighing; every night I make my bed swim, I dissolve my couch with my tears" (Ps. 6:4, 6 NASB). I now understand that God desires to wean his children from a feelings-based trust.

If we are ever going to know God intimately, we must move beyond juvenile superficiality of reliance upon our feelings to the unparalleled security in our relationship with him. His Word and promises must become our pacifier. Read his lips: "I will never leave you nor forsake you." In those difficult seasons, we must choose to walk with the Father in childlike trust and obedience. We can attend to our souls by journaling. We can write "Dear Jesus" letters, expressing our hearts to him, or we can imagine Jesus writing a letter to us. (What would he say?) This would be a good time to reread earlier journal entries to remind ourselves of God's goodness. We can pray the Scriptures and sing worship songs in a place of solitude. In addition, we can ask others to pray for us. That is a way of riding the coattails of someone else's faith when it is hard to get to God on our own.

His eye is on the sparrow. God hears our cry, and he sees our tears. In the autumn and winter of our lives, whether we feel him or not, he's there. He's not there because we feel him; he's there because he is.

God is our refuge and strength, an ever-present help [and hug] in trouble.

PSALM 46:1

CRYING OUT LOUD

Have you heard the story listing the many reasons God created mothers? I love the concluding thought, which reminds us that the most important reason God created mothers was simply because he couldn't be available physically to wipe the tear of every single child as it rolled down his or her little face. My wife's ability to tend to the tears in our home amazes me. Not only is her compassion the greatest I have ever seen, but her ability to distinguish between the many different "tear moments" is a gift I believe is specially given to mothers.

There are those cries of a newborn baby that no one can understand, yet a mother can hear her child and know if he is hungry, tired, or simply needing a swaddle and a hug. Our youngest child cried for almost a year straight. There were moments when I honestly didn't know if I could make it, yet my wife held her composure and her compassion together at every turn. She assured me that the child was bright, alert, and seeking to be a part of the bigger world around him. I couldn't see any of those traits in the wailing, and to be honest, I was thankful for grandparents and swings. But you know what? That tiny infant has turned into one of the most engaging, animated people I know. I can see now how all those hours of crying were messages from this tiny boy saying, "Hey, I'm here and I'm looking to be a part of things. Hello!" My wife—this child's mother—knew the sounds of her child's cry.

Do you cry out to God? I have to admit this is something that did not come naturally to me, and I've had to learn to go to God with my tears. Amazingly, just as a loving parent can distinguish between the cries of her child, God knows our different cries. He is waiting to respond to our tears whether they are tears of joy, suffering, sorrow, or anger.

Psalm 40 is a wonderful word picture of a man, David, who allowed God to share his tears: "I waited patiently for the LORD; And He inclined to me and heard my cry. He brought me up out of the pit of destruction, out of the miry clay, and He set my feet upon a rock making my footsteps firm. He put a new song in my mouth, a song of praise to our God; many will see and fear and will trust in the LORD" (Ps. 40:1–3 NASB).

In this passage, David was crying out to God from a valley point in his life. It isn't clear what the exact circumstances were at this time in David's life, but there is no question that David turned to God to share his grief. And what was God's response? David says God pulled him out of the depths and made his footsteps firm. David's heart was filled with praise for God, and he expressed his praise in song. What an amazing picture. We can learn from this passage of Scripture that God will hear our cry and *respond to it*. He will take the heavy burden we are carrying and replace it with surety and strength of purpose. Our faith will be strengthened in the process, and we, like David, will be filled with praise for God the Father who hears our cry and responds to us in love.

God is as eager to hear our cries of joy as he is our cries of distress and sorrow. Sometimes I think God has the job of the vice principal in the local high school. Do you remember the vice principal? He was the disciplinarian. He got to see all of the "troubled" kids on a regular basis, but he scarcely knew the names or faces of the good kids. Is this how God knows you? It's certainly more natural for me to cry out to God when I'm in the valley than when I am on my mountaintop. I have to consciously remind myself almost daily that God desires intimacy with me and wants to hear from me at every step—both high and low. I need to share all of life's moments with him, and he will do great things in and through me.

What an amazing picture of God our Father—sitting on his throne waiting to hear from me and anxious to distinguish between my cries so that he can provide comfort, guidance, and strength.

I waited patiently for the LORD . . . and [he] heard my cry.

PSALM 40:1

7

AFRAID OF THE DARK

Are you afraid of the dark? I'm not—anymore. But oh how I remember those long, long nights. There's something about being in a dark room that can be terrifying to children. The shadows make faces on the wall when the wind blows through the branches of the tree outside. Sometimes the house just squeaks for no reason anyone can explain. And then there's the ever present boogeyman. He's hiding under the bed, in the closet, or maybe even in the toy box.

When one of my little guys looks up at me at bedtime and echoes fears of the darkness, I try to reassure him, because I remember the dark so well. I put my face right next to his and say, "You know what, son? Sometimes Daddy's afraid of the dark. But when Daddy's afraid of the dark, Daddy prays to Jesus, and Jesus gives Daddy courage."

It's true, you know. I don't fear the natural darkness that my sons are reacting to, but there have been times in my life when a different kind of darkness shrouds me.

I think as adults we are afraid of the dark. We might be intimidated and terrified by the darkness that comes in the days in which we are living—the darkness of terrorist attacks and threats of terrorism. Financial changes and economic instability can cause us to have fears of the dark. Crime and incurable diseases can contribute to our fear of the dark. But just as I reassured my son, God the Father wants to reassure us.

We have a strong, constant beacon in Jesus Christ—he is our ultimate night-light. "When Jesus spoke again to the people, he said, 'I am the *light* of the *world*. Whoever follows me will never walk in darkness, but will have the *light* of life'" (John 8:12, emphasis added).

When we are living in times or hours or moments of darkness, we can have confidence. We can be "as bold as a lion" (Prov. 28:1) because Jesus is our light. His Word is a lamp unto our feet and a light unto our path. Take courage in these words—let them give you hope and light when darkness seems to envelop you.

One time I was eating lunch in the park when a loose dog suddenly started chasing a little boy who was playing near me. That little guy had the look of terror on his face as he raced to his dad. But once safely behind his dad's legs, he was the bravest man in town. "Get away from me, doggie, or I'll hurt you!"

This is what God wants to do for us. He wants us to run to him, allowing him to give us strength and courage. Proverbs 18:10 says, "The name of the LORD is a *strong tower;* the righteous run to it and are safe" (emphasis added). Just as the little boy became bold behind the strength of his father, we too can be bold. Jesus will show us the way. No matter how great the darkness, Jesus is our night-light. He is with us always, even unto the end of the world.

Hear my cry, O God; listen to my prayer. From the ends of the earth I call to you, I call as my heart grows faint; lead me to the rock that is higher than I. For you have been my refuge, a strong tower against the foe.

PSALM 61:1–3

8

CHICKEN POX
OF THE SOUL

One pox, two pox, three pox, four.
Pox on feet. Pox on arms.
Pox on face. Pox on pox.
No more pox!

We have become huge fans of the creators of calamine lotion. But even while scuba diving in the ocean of calamine lotion, our boys still suffered with chicken pox. This left us miserable. While they were still in the bathtub, going down for one last dip, Lezlyn and I decided to have a CPA (Chicken Pox Anonymous) meeting outside the door. We were powerless to stop the itching, and everyone's sleep had become unmanageable. The situation required desperate measures. They each had a part of their body that itched the most. We agreed to sacrifice sleeping in our cozy, king-size bed to sleep with them in their narrow twin-size beds.

I was assigned to our oldest boy, Johnny. His scalp was harassing him like a bee buzzing around a picnic table full of food. Dad to the rescue! I got a face towel and soaked it in cold water. I held the towel on his head all night. He slept fine the remainder of the night. I suffered from being in an awkward position. My being there and holding that cold, wet towel to his scalp, becoming incredibly uncomfortable for my child's sake, brought him comfort and healing. It brought to me a deep satisfaction that I was really loving my boy during his time of need.

As I reflect on that season in Johnny's life, my awkwardness and discomfort pale in significance when I consider how my trial lasted only one night while God's discomfort lasted several days. The Son of God suffered and died for the "chicken pox" that plagued our soul.

His great love for us led him to leave the comfort and beauty of a heavenly residence to heal our soul's "itching" problem once and for all. He who knew no sin became sin on our behalf, that we might become the righteousness of God in him.

He is the Great Physician who neither slumbers nor sleeps, still making soul (house) calls, still prescribing the right remedy that grants sleep for his beloved.

God made him who had no sin to be sin for us.

2 CORINTHIANS 5:21

9 ————————————

BREATH OF LIFE

Bedtimes are special in our home. Besides the fact that the kids are quiet and my wife and I can look forward to completing a sentence without interruption, cuddling together as we listen to music by the fireplace, or enjoying a good movie, bedtimes are a prime time to make meaningful investments in shaping our children's self-esteem and self-image. At bedtime, kids are more vulnerable than at perhaps any other part of the day. It's dark. The boogeyman and monsters have just reported in to torment them another night. Real and imagined fears surface in their young hearts. They are more apt to process their feelings about events that occurred during the course of the day.

We have a phrase in our home that we use regularly: breathe life. It comes from the Hebrew word for encouragement. It conveys the idea of applying strength to one's arms and legs in order to be able to handle pressure. We define encouragement as breathing life into one another.

We purpose to breathe life into our children through our touch and words as they lie on the bed. We heap mounds of physical affection upon them through backrubs and stroking

36

their forehead and hair. Medical research has shown that the amount of hemoglobin is significantly increased through touch. Hemoglobin is the component of the blood that carries oxygen from the lungs to the tissue and organs. Consequently, increased hemoglobin improves our ability to fight off sickness and diseases. The power of touch! When we touch our children lovingly, we literally breathe life into them.

Another way we breathe life into them is through our words. As we pray over them, we speak affirming words, such as, "You are fearfully and wonderfully made. You are beautiful inside and outside, and you are loved deeply. May God make you as trees planted by the streams of living water, and may you bring forth fruit in your season. May you be leaders of righteousness and not followers of evil." We even have them touch and pray over one another.

Death and life are in the power of the tongue (Prov. 18:21). We breathe life into our children when we lavish them with life-giving words. The power of words! Think about it—a balloon cannot soar until it has first been _____ into. (You fill in the blank!)

The first instance of breathing life into a person did not occur at a bedside but in a garden—the Garden of Eden. It was a parent-child relationship: God the Father and Adam, his child.

God has style. His style was to be up-close-and-personal. I imagine him affectionately holding Adam's face as he gently breathed life into Adam's nostrils. And Adam became what was breathed into him, namely *life*. Studies have shown that whatever we perceive the most significant person in our world to believe about us is usually the view we adopt of ourselves, whether good, bad, or ugly.

Children have a tendency to become whatever is "breathed into" them. If shame is breathed into them, they tend to become shamed people. If praise and encouragement are breathed into them, they tend to become confident people. The popular poem "Children Learn What They Live" by Dorothy Law Nolte, is really true. Let's face it. Many of us have had emotional halitosis (bad breath) breathed unto us (words) and breathed onto us (deeds) during our upbringing. This is not intended to parent-bash. Most parents do the best they know how in loving and caring for their children. But, at times, parents' best efforts to be life-breathers for their children fall short.

This is why we need to know our heavenly Father. He breathes very good stuff into his children. He resuscitates the lifeless soul. It creates within you a clean heart and renews a right spirit. He calls you "saint." He calls you "beloved." He says, "You are of more value." What a breath of fresh air!

See how very much our heavenly Father loves us, for he allows us to be called his children, and we really are!

1 JOHN 3:1 NLT

LAY YOUR HEAD
ON MY SHOULDER

Nothing in the world is more special or intimate than when I hold my infant or preschool sons and they voluntarily lay their head on my shoulder. It is a safe and cozy position for them. It is an opportunity to allow my arms, hands, and shoulder to provide a measure of security to them and to allow them to rest on me. We experience a degree of shared warmth, a degree of mutual affection that is inexplicable.

A person will not lay his head on your shoulder when he does not feel safe. When one of my sons lays his head on my shoulder and melts in my arms, I sense he is communicating to me, nonverbally but loud and clear nonetheless, "I feel safe with you, Dad; I know you are not going to hurt me." He is relying on me to hold him, to protect him, to rock him to sleep. Again, you cannot sleep where you do not feel safe. When my sons are willing to rest on me, they are affirming that I am a safe person in their eyes.

Even as a teenager, Isaac knew this kind of safety in his relationship with his father, Abraham. When Isaac was taken to Mount Moriah to be sacrificed and killed (unbeknownst to him)

FAITH LIKE A CHILD

and was laid on the altar with the kindling wood beneath his helpless body, I do not believe he squirmed. Listen to the question he had asked his father earlier: "Where is the lamb for the burnt offering?" (Gen. 22:7 NASB). Abraham had assured Isaac that God would provide a sacrifice. We need the kind of track record with our loved ones that when we give them an answer, they do not feel a need to ask for extensive details.

Certainly Isaac never in his wildest dreams thought he would be the one his devoted father would sacrifice to the Lord. I imagine him thinking, "You are my dad, and I trust you not to hurt me. I rest in the security of your love."

It is one thing for an infant, a preschooler, or even an adolescent to lay his head on his daddy's shoulders, but what about a man? Can a man lay his head on his Lord's shoulders? Does he ever outgrow this? Is it normal or appropriate?

The Bible contains a vignette about John, one of the Lord's disciples, which may shed light on those questions. John did not think that resting his head on someone's shoulder was something to be feared or something that a man outgrows. During the Lord's Supper, "There was reclining on Jesus' bosom one of His disciples, whom Jesus loved" (John 13:23 NASB).

Why does a man require the Lord's shoulder for a place to lay his head? It seems to me that it is for the same reasons that my children require my shoulders for resting their heads. My sons desire my shoulders for rest when they are tired and for comfort when they are in pain. Sometimes they do not realize they are tired, and I, like the shepherd in Psalm 23:2, must make them lie down.

Men sometimes feel a tiredness that is not merely a result of physical overexertion or lack of sleep but from emotional and spiritual weariness. It is a tiredness resulting from their spiritual walk, from always giving when the situation demands it, and/or from their being mostly disconnected from themselves and their fellow men.

Unfortunately, as men, we are sometimes too macho to lay our heads on Jesus' shoulders. Or it may be that we do not trust his shoulders and hands to hold us. Jesus did not say to John, "Don't you think you are a little too big for this, John?" No. Nor did he ask, "Do you realize this is gender inappropriate behavior?" No. Jesus was really comfortable and secure with who he was and with the way John related to him.

A shoulder acts as a sort of hanger. A hanger is used to support clothes. The Lord gives us his shoulders on which to hang the garments of our weariness and our pain. He does not *make* us rest, but he does provide a place where we can rest securely and sleep in safety. He does not keep us from pain, but he promises to be with us in the pain. In fact, that is his name: *Immanuel, God with us.* God's shoulder is always available to us, beckoning us to simply come. For far too long, almost since the beginning of time, men and women have opted to lay their heads in the lap of a seductor, or rest their heads on the La-Z-Boy recliner while watching television, or live it up, only to find themselves with hangovers brought on by substance abuse. All these pretenders are only artificial comforters and temporary relaxers who pull a bait-and-switch con job. They promise more than they can deliver. They appear on the outside to be soft, over-stuffed pillows upon which we can relax our heads, but they are really filled with dynamite designed for our doom. John felt a weariness for which he needed the shoulders of the God of all comfort to support him.

Another hero of the faith, Moses, found that when his strength grew small, he had to rely on Aaron and Hur to hold his arms up (Exod. 17:12). They were like shoulders for him.

We all need people who love us and who are willing to hold us up. But even these relationships have their limits. People do get weary. Jesus beckons us to come unto him. I can think of no better way to encourage you than to lean on the arms that are able.

Come to me, all you who are weary and burdened, and I will give you rest.

MATTHEW 11:28

11

NO MORE BLANKIE

Remember Linus from *Peanuts*? He was the one with the blankie permanently attached to his side. That blankie went everywhere Linus went, from the bedroom to the table to the playground, and even to the classroom. Linus, quite literally, couldn't function without his blankie.

I found myself thinking about Linus as I watched my son Jordan develop an attachment to his blankie. It started as a "crib only" thing—something he wanted at nap time or bedtime—but it soon developed into an accessory for every outfit he owned. The blankie had to go everywhere Jordan went. It gave him comfort and made him feel secure. Try as we might, my wife and I couldn't seem to wean Jordan away from that one, special blankie.

While Jordan's blankie was harmless, it was a false comforter. It was merely an object that Jordan turned to for immediate comfort. Spiritually speaking, a child's blankie symbolizes an adult version of an idol—something we run to for comfort when we feel pain or unrest. Just as Jordan felt pain and turned to his blankie for comfort, the Christian can feel pain or fear and turn to an unhealthy practice, object, or relationship for comfort.

What are some "blankies" that we run to for comfort?

- Food is a big one for many people. They aren't a bit hungry, but they eat because it makes them feel better emotionally.
- On the flip side, exercise can be a blankie. It gives people an outlet for their emotions temporarily but does not provide permanent peace.
- Work is a place that many of us run to escape our fears or pain. We dig in, focus on our objectives, and hope the discomfort will go away. At the end of the day, we find the same pain in our heart that was there in the beginning.
- Unhealthy relationships plague people universally. People think the answer to their pain lies in a friend or lover. Too often, this results in further heartache.

Jordan finally gave up his blankie after a night of stomach flu. He got so sick, he threw up all over it. He had to give it up to be cleaned and let his mom and me lovingly nurse him back to wellness. From that night on, Jordan didn't want the blankie anymore. He had learned that his mother and father could comfort him more completely than anything else. He learned to allow us to provide him love and security in his times of need.

God wants us to turn to him for comfort. He'll allow us to wander off course. He'll even allow us a grown-up version of Jordan's flu night to remind us of our need for him. But he would much rather have us choose to stay on course at all times. The next time you find yourself wavering toward your blankie, crawl into the arms of your loving Father and allow him to give you the rest you so deeply desire.

Dear children, keep yourselves from idols.

1 JOHN 5:21

12

HEAVEN IS SWEETER
THAN CANDY

I have been described as a sensitive man, but I never cried more in one day than when I conducted the funeral of nine-year-old Erika Smith, who was brutally murdered along with her father. I was filled with the normal shock and disbelief that this tragedy was a reality. I said to myself, this young girl is about the same age as one of my own sons. I wrestled with the same questions that many of you have faced: How did this senseless tragedy happen? Why did this happen to one so young? If God is love, where was he when this happened?

I do not have answers to these baffling questions with which we have all wrestled as we looked at such tragedies in life. I'm not trying to defend God either. I personally believe it is highly inappropriate for anyone to attempt to answer the question "Why?" It is equally inappropriate to attempt to defend God, because God is quite capable of defending himself, thank you. He makes it clear in his Word that his ways are not our ways. He says, "I am near the brokenhearted; I save those who are crushed in spirit." I realize that God is able to handle my pain, confusion, anger, and sorrow. He knows my frame—that I am but dust. He also wants us to know that nothing can separate us from his love. Knowing all these things, we are more than conquerors through him who loves us. "Neither death nor life, neither angels nor demons, neither the present nor the future, nor any powers, neither height nor depth, nor anything else in all creation, will be able to separate us from the love of God that is in Christ Jesus" (Rom. 8:38–39).

When my two older boys saw Erika's picture on her obituary, they began to ask about her. When they saw her picture in the newspaper, they asked further questions about how this had happened to her. Their questions showed that they felt understandably insecure. Where were her parents when this happened? Where is Erika now? Did she do something wrong? Can you protect us, Dad?

I tried to tell them about Erika's life and love for Jesus and that she was with Jesus in heaven. They then wanted to know what heaven is like. Have you ever tried to explain to a ten-year-old or a six-year-old what heaven is like? I began explaining it to them in language, terms, and experiences that they know to be true. After years of experience as a dad, I have learned that children such as my sons love sweet stuff. In addition, they love playing, riding their bikes, and playing Nintendo. So I began talking to them about the realities of heaven by saying, "Guys, you know how you love candy and gum and all these things? You know how you love riding your bike and playing baseball and playing Nintendo?"

As I expected, they answered, "Yeah, yeah, yeah, Dad. We like that stuff." Having gotten their attention, I continued.

"Well, heaven is a hundred times better than all of that stuff. It is a place where you are going to have fun, a place where you will laugh and play, where you will sing and worship God. That is what this precious little girl, Erika, is doing right now. She is singing; she is laughing; and she is playing. It is a place where there are no murders, where everyone is perfect.

"It is a place where you do not get rejections from other boys and girls. You do not have to worry about getting rejected when you try out for a basketball team. You are always on God's team. You will always be loved—always, always, always, forever and ever and ever and ever. It is sweeter than candy, guys.

And that is why it is so important that you have a relationship with Jesus Christ, so that we as a family can all be there and enjoy God forever.

"There will be no more tests in school. You just enjoy being in the presence of God and Jesus. And yet, guys, today we do feel sad because we miss Erika. Her mommy misses her. She loved her very, very much. That is why God says it is so important that we remember our Creator in the days of our youth.

"Even though we miss Erika, we want to remember what God's Word tells us. We are not to 'grieve as those who have no hope.' We believe that Jesus died and rose again, and so we believe that God will bring with Jesus those who have died before he returns."

For the Lord himself will come down from heaven, with a loud command . . . and the dead in Christ will rise first. After that, we who are still alive and are left will be caught up together with them in the clouds . . . so we will be with the Lord forever.

1 THESSALONIANS 4:16–17

13

NAP TIME

My middle son could still take a nap every day—and he's six! He has always been wired this way. As an infant, he was a two-a-day napper. My oldest son, on the other hand, resisted napping right from the very beginning.

I've discovered that this fight is familiar to most parents. No matter how desperately a child might need a nap—and don't we all know how those days go—he kicks and screams all the way to the bed, afraid he's going to miss something. He just doesn't see any fun—or use—in taking a nap.

Isn't this just like us as adults when it comes to *the nap?* Now, I don't mean nap in the traditional sense—like falling asleep in front of the football game. Actually, as adults, those kinds of naps are often high on our list of favorite things to do! When I say *the nap,* I mean rest, renewal, and time to reflect. We keep going and going and going, almost as if we are on autopilot. We start reacting to life instead of proactively choosing a path that God has laid out for us. Generally, things end up in a bit of a mess.

Psalm 23 says of the shepherd that "he *makes* me lie down in green pastures" (v. 2, emphasis added). I wonder sometimes if the shepherd really does have to make us lie down. Maybe lying down for us is when he allows a headache or an upset stomach to creep into our day. We have to lie down because we can't function.

It's said of God that he worked six days, and on the seventh day he rested. Even one of the Ten Commandments says that we should honor the Sabbath—taking a day of rest. God wants us to recreate and take time for re-creation (where we get our word *recreation*). This flows out of rest, of nap times, of sitting by the lake and reflecting. Think about when Mary and Martha were with Jesus. Martha was frustrated and angry with him—with God. "Lord, Lord, make my sister help me." I can envision Martha in the kitchen preparing to do wonderful things for Jesus, whereas Mary was in the living room sitting at his feet, drinking in his words. I just picture Jesus saying, "Oh, Martha, Martha, you worry about so many things, but Mary has chosen a good and perfect thing." What was that one thing she had chosen? To sit at his feet and to rest.

Jesus gives us an invitation. He says in Matthew 11:28, "Come to me all you who are weary and burdened, and I will give you rest." So, let's purpose to take the time to seek renewal, recreation, and reflection. In his love, sometimes he will simply have to make us lie down. But thank God, it's not in muddy patches but rather in green pastures.

The Lord is my shepherd. . . . He makes me lie down in green pastures, he leads me beside quiet waters, he restores my soul.

PSALM 23:1–3

14

LET'S PLAY PRETEND

Okay, I'm really going to date myself here and tell you that when I was a child, I wanted to be Underdog. Do you remember him? Well, that's probably just as well. Let's just say that he was one of the superheroes of my day—banished to the annals of television history now. For my youngest boy, it's Superman. "Oh, Daddy, I'm Superman. I can leap buildings in a single bound!" Caped with a towel from the linen closet, he sticks his arms out from his sides and "flies" around the house, zooming from room to room, taking corners in a clean sweep, leaping down five stairs at a time. . . . It's a bird, it's a plane . . . it's Joel! Somehow I really think Joel feels bigger and more powerful when he is in the midst of his Superman game.

Have you ever engaged in a grown-up version of "Let's Pretend"? Just like our children, it's not uncommon for us to try to convince ourselves and those around us that we are something that we are not.

Maybe we're trying to pretend we have more money than we really do just to "keep up with the Joneses." We buy a fancy new car that will catch the neighbor's eye with its sparkle—but

FAITH LIKE A CHILD

we have more month than money at the end of every pay cycle. But hey, it's just a game of pretend.

Maybe we want everyone to think we have the perfect marriage. We go to church, holding hands with our spouse or with our arms wrapped around each other because it's the thing to do. But we really don't like each other very much at all, and in fact, our marriage is anything but healthy. But it's the perception that's important—and it's just a game of pretend.

The Pharisees were engaged in a life of pretend. Jesus was so frustrated with them that he called them whitewashed tombs. He said, "You are like whitewashed tombs, which look beautiful on the outside but on the inside are full of dead men's bones and everything unclean . . . on the outside you appear to people as righteous but on the inside you are full of hypocrisy and wickedness" (Matt. 23:27–28). Jesus' message is clear—it doesn't matter how beautiful the outside is if the inside is full of guck. In games of pretend, all of us can make the outside of our marriages, our bodies, and our financial situation look attractive, but the real deal is what's going on inside our hearts. This is what God cares about.

The Bible challenges us to live authentic lives, and in Galatians 6:3 we are taught, "If anyone thinks he is something when he is nothing, he deceives himself." God created us, and he knows that we're not Superman, Wonder Woman, or Super-Couple. He calls us to a life of humility and a life of truth. In an authentic life, what you see is what you get. There is no deception, no cover-up, and no grand game of "Let's Pretend."

Let no man deceive himself.

1 CORINTHIANS 3:18 NASB

15

MINE, MINE, MINE

Years ago, before I had children of my own, I remember reading a short vignette titled the *Toddler's Creed*. It went like this:

If I want it, it's mine.
If I give it to you and change my mind later, it's mine.
If I can take it away from you, it's mine.
If I had it a little while ago, it's mine.
If it's mine, it will never belong to anyone else, no matter what.
If we are building something together, all the pieces are mine.
If it looks just like mine, it's mine.

Author Unknown

These words didn't mean anything to me at the time, but after watching my three boys go through the toddler years, I have new respect and understanding for the person who authored those words. Children are selfish. It's woven in them at birth in a way we can't possibly understand until we see it unfold before our very eyes.

It took me a little while to catch on. My firstborn could do no wrong in those early days. He had this little stuffed bear that sang when you wound the key. The boy could barely talk when he started bringing it to me to wind, but the minute that bear started singing, John-John would put his arms up and coo, "Mine, mine, mine." I thought it was so *cute* that he knew the bear was his and could get the word out of his mouth not once, not twice, but three times!

My wife tried to tell me at the time that this was not a good thing and certainly not one to note proudly on John-John's list of accomplishments. But to be honest, it took me a while longer to begin to see her point. It really wasn't until our second son was born that my foggy veil began to clear. Suddenly all those *mine*s looked a little different. The stuffed bear? "Mine!" The rocking chair? "Mine!" The baby's bottle? "Mine!" And on and on it went. The little guy was a *mine* field—and it was not a good thing.

In these moments of observing my son and thinking about my own heart, it became oh so clear to me that indeed, we are each born with a selfish heart. It is in our nature to think of ourselves first and foremost, and we must work diligently to unlearn this natural trait.

When God goes that extra mile to make sure we understand something, I take that as confirmation that the issue is one of which I need to be very conscious. Selfishness is one of those issues. We are instructed countless times in God's Word to put others first in our minds and in our hearts. Why? Because we have Christ as our model—the ultimate servant. In Philippians 2:4, Paul says, "Each of you should look not only to your own interests, but also to the interests of others." He follows this in verse 5 with, "Your attitude should be the same as that of Christ Jesus."

We are instructed to love our brother as ourselves. Why? Because God knows of our inborn, self-focused nature. He wants us to draw on that love of self and use it to pour out love to others. The amazing thing is that if we will work diligently to become unselfish, our blessings will multiply in ways we cannot fathom because there is joy in sharing and giving to others.

Madeleine L'Engle, in her book *Irrational Season*, summed up this miraculous change so well: "The most difficult thing to let go is my *self*, that self which coddled and cozened, becomes smaller as it becomes heavier. I don't understand how and why I come to *be* only as I lose myself, but I know from long experience that this is so." You see, while we are wired to be selfish, it is only when we truly learn to be selfless that our heart experiences its greatest joy and contentment. Pretty amazing.

I saw this principle at work the other day in my sons. They came home from school and told me that one of their friends forgot his lunch. My boys love to eat, especially potato chips, but they shared their chips and drink with the other little boy because they just couldn't bear to see him go without lunch. My heart skipped a beat as they finished telling me every detail of the lunchroom scene. As a father, my heart was moved by their generosity.

God's heart is moved when we share our chips and drink with those around us. Do you remember the little boy who shared his lunch with Jesus and how he took that bread and fish and fed a multitude? When we offer our "lunch" to Jesus, we are blessed in ways we can't even begin to imagine, and many lives beyond our own are touched. But when we horde, keeping our "lunch" to ourselves no matter the needs around us, we miss out on the privilege of all that God has in store for us.

My heart is inclined to want to live out the *Toddler's Creed*, but I am a work in progress. I know that if I keep focused, God and I together can overcome my selfish nature, keeping me out of the *mine* field and on the path of becoming more and more like Christ.

Each of you should look not only to your own interests, but also to the interests of others. Your attitude should be the same as that of Christ Jesus.

PHILIPPIANS 2:4–5

16

GRACE AND SOILED DIAPERS

Some dear friends of ours have three children ages twelve, ten, and nine, and they are a great family. It really is a wonderful gift to have your children that close together—but oh the diapers they used to go through! I remember the harried days in their house when the third child was born. The oldest child hadn't turned three yet; he wasn't toilet trained, and so he continued in the diaper brigade with his two young sisters. To be honest, I can't even imagine!

Luckily for all of us, the exact number of diapers we've changed for each of our children is a secret that no one will ever know. Why? Because when we welcome a new baby into our lives, we know that diapers are part of the deal. It is an expected and necessary part of a child's development.

If there is one thing I have learned through my parenting years, it's that every child is completely and totally different, and yes, this even reaches into the mundane world of soiled diapers. Now infants communicate the message, "Hey, I need a clean diaper over here!" by crying. But when that magical age of toddlerhood arrives, everything changes.

There are those few magical toddlers who come to you immediately and actually ask you, in their own special way, to clean them up. Ahh, I remember having one of those! He would not only come to his mother or me asking, but he would lie quietly through the whole changing-of-the-diaper process.

It's not always so easy though. There are those children who want to keep their dirty work a secret. They may go into a private place with the hope that you won't ever find out they need a cleaning, and then, once discovered, they have the audacity to wrestle with you as you attempt to change their diaper. Eventually you win out, but oh the struggle! Does it really have to be this hard?

Now stop for a minute and think about the parallel between our role in the diaper-changing arena and God's role as the parent in our lives. Imagine God's reaction when we dirty ourselves through our words, our attitudes, and our behaviors. Imagine the stench in God's nostrils as we muck up our relationships just one more time. Yet his heart's desire is to clean us up so we can be a sweet-smelling aroma in the world. "For we are to God the aroma of Christ among those who are being saved and those who are perishing" (2 Cor. 2:15).

Just as the toddler must accept the fact that he needs to be cleaned up, so must we accept that we've made a mess before God can clean us up. Beyond accepting it in our own mind and heart, we must confess our wrong before God. His Word says, "If we confess our sins, he is faithful and just and will forgive us our sins and purify us from all unrighteousness" (1 John 1:9). There is no private place we can run in hopes of hiding our sin, for whatever is done in the dark will come to light. Just as the toddler's soiled diaper gives him away, the Bible says, "You may be sure that your sin will find you out" (Num. 32:23).

The most wonderful part of God our Father is that he is waiting for us to run to him when we have an "oops." He's not waiting with his record book, thinking, "Oh boy, here he comes again. Will he ever learn?" Why? Because just as we don't keep count of the number of diapers we changed for each of our chil-

FAITH LIKE A CHILD

dren's messes, God doesn't keep count of the cleanups he's had to be involved in on our behalf. He knows that spiritual diapers are part of the deal as we work to become more like Christ.

In him we have redemption through his blood, the forgiveness of sins, in accordance with the riches of God's grace that he lavished on us with all wisdom and understanding.

EPHESIANS 1:7–8

56

17

LOVE LAB

Typically, before traveling apart from my family, I gather my boys together and give them a little pep talk: "Mommy is Daddy's girlfriend. Mommy was Daddy's girlfriend before you were born. Mommy is Daddy's girlfriend while you're here, and Mommy will be Daddy's girlfriend when you grow up and move away from here. Honor and listen to Mommy while Daddy is gone."

By this time, they usually have a deer-in-the-headlights look as they nod and say, "Yes, Dad." I remind them that they are princes, and Mommy is the queen, which makes me you-know-who. I tell them that one day they will grow up to be kings and marry queens. Until then, they are to honor Queen Mommy.

King Solomon gave solid counsel to his son about marriage when he told him, "He who finds a wife finds what is good" (Prov. 18:22). I want my boys to realize that we are not raising them simply to date girls. We want them to date and mate as God sees fit. We want them to find his "good thing" for their lives. I tell them how we got a head start the moment they were born. It was then we began praying for their future spouses.

Another practice we observe is to conduct impromptu interviews with three- and six-year-old girls at church nurseries wherever we go. These girls are invited to participate in a good-natured, spiritual assessment inventory, take a battery of psychological tests, and provide three character references. (Hey, you can never be sure. We're simply testing the waters and showing our boys how to evaluate prospective mates.)

We want our boys to have a positive view of marriage. Our home is the laboratory where they observe, ask questions, and conduct experiments pertaining to wholesome relationships. They take notes on how a man treats his lady and how a woman cares for her man. So I make sure they get good practice attending to Queen Mommy—holding the door for her, praying over her, telling her she looks beautiful (which always seems to get me in trouble). As they get older, Mommy will take them on dates and instruct them on how to be extraordinary men in their relationships with women.

Two penetrating questions we constantly ask ourselves are, "Am I (Johnny) becoming the kind of man I want my sons to be?" and "Am I (Lezlyn) becoming the kind of woman I want my sons to marry?" These questions act as guardrails to help keep us on the road heading in the right direction.

A couple of years ago, the pastor of a church we attended invited all the children to come up front during the worship service. He asked the children this question, "What happens when you get married?" Our oldest son (who was four at the time) enthusiastically blurted out, "You dance and buy flowers."

Great answer! Whew. There are many other answers he could have given, some of which might have been somewhat embarrassing. This kid earned an A from his internship in the Parker love lab.

Listen, my sons, to a father's instruction; pay attention and gain understanding.

PROVERBS 4:1

58

18

A TIME TO WEEP

I'm fond of the story about the young girl who took a while returning from the candy store. Her worried mother met her at the door and inquired, "Sweetheart, what took you so long?"

The girl replied, "I saw a little girl crying because her doll baby was broken."

The mother said, "That was nice of you to stop to help her fix it."

"No, Mommy," said the girl. "I stopped to cry with her."

Following dinner one evening, we observed a similar experience with our boys. It wasn't a broken doll. Rather, it was a sore head. While playing together, Jordan watched as his older brother, Johnny, inadvertently bumped his head against the wall and began crying. Jordan, sensing his brother's pain, started crying as well. However, Jordan did not stop there. He immediately sought out Mom and Dad to inform us of Johnny's mishap.

Empathy. This is precisely what the Father means when he commands us to "weep with those who weep" (hurt with those who hurt). This is in striking contrast to rejoicing in someone else's pain and silently wishing failure upon them in order that we may feel better about ourselves. When I think of empathy,

I think of putting into practice one of God's greatest commandments: "Love one another. As I have loved you, so you must love one another" (John 13:34).

God's command to love others as he loves us is no small instruction. In fact, it is repeated over and over again in the Scriptures. Let's take a look at just a few examples:

- "Be devoted to one another in brotherly love. Honor one another above yourselves" (Rom. 12:10).
- "Be completely humble and gentle; be patient, bearing with one another in love" (Eph. 4:2).
- "This is the message you heard from the beginning: We should love one another" (1 John 3:11).
- "And this is his command: to believe in the name of his Son, Jesus Christ, and to love one another as he commanded us" (1 John 3:23).
- "Dear friends, since God so loved us, we also ought to love one another" (1 John 4:11).

When God repeats something time and time again, two thoughts come to mind. The first is that the message God is trying to get across to me is of the utmost importance—he wants to make sure I get it. The second is that God *knows* how difficult the task at hand is—so he repeats himself more than a few times to make sure I get it.

To be honest, being an empathetic person, one who reaches out and responds to others in love, is something I've had to work at. I think it came quite naturally to me as a young child, much as it did to my son when his brother hit his head. But somewhere along the road to becoming an adult, my heart began to harden. It wasn't that I woke up one day and decided I wasn't going to practice empathy anymore. It was more a gradual "bucking up" that happened over the years.

I see it in my children. While the youngest will reach out to anyone and everyone with his heart on his sleeve, the middle son is less inclined to do so, and the oldest is even less so. Life has a way of doing this to all of us, starting when we're very young, because the world in which we live doesn't encourage us to love others as ourselves. It is a cutthroat place where people are trained to look out for number one. With enough encouragement and practice, looking out for number one replaces any instinct we might have to look out for the other person first. As a parent, I have to train my boys to make a conscious effort not to be swayed by the world. As a Christian father, husband, and brother, I have to check my own heart to make sure I am reaching out to others in love—the same love that God has for me.

Beyond being empathetic, God calls us to intercede on behalf of others. "I urge, then, first of all, that requests, prayers, intercession and thanksgiving be made for everyone—for kings and all those in authority, that we may live peaceful and quiet lives in all godliness and holiness" (1 Tim. 2:1–2).

When Johnny hit his head that day, Jordan not only felt his pain (empathy), he sought out Mom and Dad for help. Jordan was mirroring what the Father has in mind when he tells us to intercede for others. When we see people in need, God intends for us to seek him out on their behalf. This might take the form of prayer for a brokenhearted friend, a meal for a family going through a stretch of unemployment, or a weekend of child care for a couple in desperate need of time away to resuscitate their marriage. God's direction isn't specific as to what our intercession should look like, but he is clear that we are to avoid pursuing our own interests exclusively. Loving others as God loves us directly connects to putting that love into action. Think of God providing the Holy Spirit to intercede for us when we are in desperate need. He loved us so much that he sent the Spirit to be with us at every moment of every day. He put action behind his words, and we must do the same. Living a life of love is challenging, but we are up to the task if we remember that God is with us every step of the way.

Rejoice with those who rejoice; mourn with those who mourn.

ROMANS 12:15

19

DIVING IN

My boys and I were trying to escape the hot, humid summer weather by taking a swim at a local pool. As I watched, my oldest son headed for the diving board. To be honest, this made me a little nervous. I knew he was a pretty good swimmer—in the shallow section of the pool! He had spent the better part of the day where the water was only three feet deep. In this safe zone, his confidence had soared because his head was well above the waterline, and he felt no worries. Filled with this new confidence, and a lot of curiosity, he had decided to head for the diving board—where the water was a good ten to twelve feet deep.

I could see that my boy really wanted to try this whole diving board thing. Part of me wanted to say, "No, I don't want you to do it. It just isn't safe because you aren't ready." But the other part of me said, "Yeah, go ahead. Try it. You'll be fine." The lifeguards were nearby—his mother wasn't—so I gave my okay.

Up the ladder he climbed, taking a look around, giving a shrug, as if to say, "What's the big deal?" and off he went. My heart took a leap, and I instantly sent a quick prayer up to God as I watched him go into that water. Then, there he was, swimming. I was so thrilled for him, excited that he had taken this leap of faith.

Hebrews 11:6 says, "Without faith it is impossible to please God." Going through life, it's easy to stay in the shallow water, that place where you feel confident and don't feel the need for a lifeguard nearby just in case. Maybe it's in your job, your Bible study, your relationships, or your piano playing. You don't stretch yourself because you're confident. You know how to do it the way you've been doing it, and to be honest, that feels good.

Unfortunately, staying in our comfort zone doesn't stretch us, grow us, or help us learn new life skills. Many times God will invade our safe place because we have grown complacent. He wants us to grow and develop. He is excited when we are willing to take a risk, to move into a new territory, to conquer a new land.

Luke 2:52 says, "And Jesus grew in wisdom and stature, and in favor with God and men." Isn't that amazing? Naturally, in the course of a physical life, Jesus would grow in stature. That is simply growing taller. But grow in wisdom? That implies Jesus took where he had been and what he had experienced and used them as he moved forward. This is our challenge. Take the experiences of where we have been and learn from them. Did we handle that correctly? Could we have done it differently? What did God want us to learn from this situation? How can we apply this lesson? If we are too content to stay on our same old path, we can't fully grow into the person God has designed us to be.

In addition to gaining wisdom through discernment, stepping off the diving board requires simple faith. Remember in the Book of Matthew when Jesus walked on water? Jesus had just finished feeding the five thousand. He sent the disciples ahead of him while he dismissed the crowd and went into the mountains to pray. "During the fourth watch of the night Jesus went out to [the disciples], walking on the lake. When the disciples saw him . . . they were terrified. . . . But Jesus immediately said to them: 'Take courage! It is I. Don't be afraid'" (Matt. 14:25–27).

Peter wasn't so sure this ghost was Jesus. He said, "Lord, if it's you, tell me to come to you on the water" (v. 28).

"Come," Jesus replied (v. 29).

Peter stepped out of the boat and began to walk on the water. But when he saw the wind, he was afraid and called out. Jesus caught him, saying, "You of little faith, why did you doubt?" (v. 31).

It excited Jesus when Peter asked to walk on the water, and Peter had faith that Jesus would allow him this privilege. But the minute Peter's faith was shaken, he began to lose his step. He called out to Jesus in his moment of weakness.

"Faith is being sure of what we hope for and certain of what we do not see" (Heb. 11:1). Faith is walking in obedience to what God has said even when we don't see it. It's walking in obedience to what God has spoken, even though we don't feel it. It's taking a risk, stepping out on a limb because we trust that God will meet us there.

In a real sense, the lifeguards and I were like Jesus to my son on that day. If he struggled and did not come up from that water, the lifeguards and I would have been right in there to rescue him. Take a dive today. What is God calling you to dive into, to step out in faith on, to walk on water toward him? The key is faith that has its eyes on the living God, and that's Jesus. My son looked at me and those lifeguards, and he felt assurance. With our eyes on Jesus, we can be assured. The Lord is our helper—we can do all things through him.

Let us fix our eyes on Jesus, the author and perfecter of our faith.

HEBREWS 12:2

64

20

JUST BECAUSE

When each of my children was born, I remember being amazed in a goofy way at the little things. When they sneezed, it didn't bother them in the least because, somehow, they knew it was normal. The hiccups got the same reaction. Do you remember how many times your kids got the hiccups in those first few weeks? Sometimes they would last so long I would start to wonder if everything was okay, but again, they weren't bothered. No tears, no squalling. Just a "blcchup" and on to the next thing.

Watching them, I was struck by their simple faith. Now I know that it's impossible to know what babies are thinking when they hiccup or sneeze. Actually, I'm not even sure they think about it at all. But isn't that the point? They are so secure in their place that they don't give these blurps a second thought. If they were frightened or unsure, they would communicate this to me or their mom by crying. I honestly think they just consider it part of the deal and trust, in their baby way, that all is fine.

This is the kind of faith I want to have in God. I want to get to the point that I am going through life without second-guessing every little detail—the hiccups—of my life. I believe without a doubt that God calls us to a life of faith. In fact, I believe God's actions in my life have a direct connection to the faith I have in him.

In Matthew 9 we read the story of the two blind men. They had amazing faith. Do you remember how they followed Jesus through the crowd, calling, "Have mercy on us, Son of David!" (v. 27)? In those days there was no compassion for the blind. These two men were probably spit on, both literally and figuratively. In the crowd, that day, they were probably shoved aside as people bellowed, "Get out of the way!" Yet they persevered. Why? Because they knew without a doubt that Jesus, the Son of God, could heal them.

When Jesus entered a house, the two men followed him in. Just think about that! They didn't even let a door or someone's privacy stop them. Turning to them, Jesus asked, "Do you believe that I am able to do this?" (v. 28).

They replied, "Yes, Lord" (v. 28).

Jesus "touched their eyes and said, 'According to your faith will it be done to you'; and their sight was restored" (vv. 29–30). *According to your faith . . .*

Further in Matthew, Jesus returns to his hometown of Nazareth. Teaching in the synagogue, Jesus garners quite a reaction from the townspeople. "Where did this man get this wisdom and these miraculous powers? . . . Isn't this the carpenter's son? Isn't his mother's name Mary . . . ? Where then did this man get all these things?" (Matt. 13:54–56). The locals are filled with questions about how this local boy, this carpenter's son, could possibly be teaching and performing miracles. Verse 57 says, "They took offense at him."

Jesus' reaction teaches us another key lesson about faith. "And he did not do many miracles there because of their lack of faith" (Matt. 13:58). *According to your faith . . .*

What is faith? Hebrews teaches us that faith is believing in what we cannot see. Chapter 11 has been referred to as the Faith Hall of Fame because it notes men and women throughout the Bible who chose to live a life based on faith. This chapter starts out defining faith for us: "Now faith is being sure of what we hope for and certain of what we do not see." And before listing the honorees, it clarifies that "this [faith] is what the ancients were commended for" (Heb. 11:1–2). Just read through the names on the list of faith heroes: Abel, Enoch, Noah, Abraham, Isaac, Jacob, Joseph, Moses' parents, Moses himself, Rahab, and on and on the list goes.

I want to be a faith hero. I want to choose to put my trust in God time and time again, because I know that by choosing faith, I am choosing a reward that will last into eternity.

Now faith is being sure of what we hope for and certain of what we do not see.

HEBREWS 11:1

21 ——

THE TRUST GAME

One night, sitting in church, I remember hearing the pastor tell a story he called *The Trust Game.*

In our house, one of the favorite things to play right before bed is "The Trust Game." It goes something like this: My girls, one by one, jump off of the stairs into my waiting arms. We start with the first stair. I say, "Jump!" At first, they look at me in wonder, completely baffled at what I'm asking them to do. I say, "Jump. It's okay. I'll catch you." They're standing so near me that we almost touch. They look at me one more time and then, with a little hop, land safely in my arms. We go to the next step and repeat the whole process.

The first couple of stairs are pretty easy because the steps are low to the ground and the girls are very near to me. But as we approach about step number three, things begin to change. The kids realize they are higher up, and they begin to lean forward to the point that they can touch me before letting themselves fall into my arms.

When we get to steps five or six, it's a completely different experience. The jumper can no longer reach out and touch me. I have caught her every time, but now the stakes are higher. The launchpad is higher, and there is free fall involved. It's a long way to the bottom, but I've caught them every time. What to do—do the girls rely on their built-up trust or let their fear stop the game?

This is exactly how my relationship with God has been throughout my life. God tends not to take us to the fifth floor of faith and then say, "Trust me." He demonstrates his trustworthiness on the first floor.

I remember going through graduate school, studying to become a counselor. By this time in my life, I had married and my first son was a newborn baby. It was a challenging time for both my wife and me, but I assured her—and myself too—that things would get better once I was finished with school. And they did—for a little while. I was offered a job at a prestigious counseling clinic, and they paid me the highest salary I had ever earned. For the next six months life couldn't have been better. And then it happened. The clinic experienced financial woes and began downsizing. Gone was the salary, and my dreams shattered right along with it. I was angry and found myself wondering where God was in all of this. I was lost and felt like I was teetering on the edge of my faith. I desperately wanted out of this trial, but God wanted me to go through it in order to build a spiritual resume called faith and trust.

Eventually, as he always does, God showed me the small window he had left open when the door of the clinic slammed shut. This time was not easy, but I know that I am a stronger man for the experience. These faith-building steps stretch and grow us. Usually we don't realize what is happening until we are far beyond the trial, but these times allow God to lead us to greater heights in our faith. Because he caught us as we jumped from the first, second, fourth, and twentieth steps, we know he will catch us from the hundredth. His faithfulness is unfailing; his love is wider and deeper than we can ever understand.

Some trust in chariots and some in horses, but we trust in the name of the Lord our God.

PSALM 20:7

22

COUNTDOWN
TO OBEDIENCE

During the beautiful spring months in my home state of Maryland, my wife and I spend many hours at local parks with our boys. Not only is this a great family time, but it is an amazing learning lab for parent-child interaction. On one of our recent outings, I was drawn in by something I have never noticed before—the countdown to obedience.

A little girl was playing on the jungle gym when her mother called to her that it was time to leave. Apparently not hearing her, the child continued playing. Her mother called her twice more, but there was still no response. Finally, completely irritated, her mother bellowed, *"Jasmine Michelle, get over here now! I'm going to count to three, one . . . two . . ."*

There it was—the countdown to obedience. Why is it that we parents develop this terrible habit? We ask our children to do something, and when they don't respond, we invoke their *complete* name (Jasmine Michelle) and begin the countdown. Usually, right before we get to "three," the child does what we were asking. Imagine that! The children buy themselves just a little more time before obeying *because they know that they can.* We have trained them to wait for the count. They know it will come, and they also know that no serious consequences will result as long as they comply before "three."

As a dad, I am guilty of playing the counting game, but it wasn't until I saw it played out in front of me at the park that I really got it. Not only am I allowing my boys to temporarily disobey, but I am teaching them a lesson of much greater significance—that God will count to three.

The truth is that God is not the inventor of the countdown to obedience, and he certainly is not a fan of this kind of game. When God has a rule for our life, he does three things:

1. He clearly states what the rule is.
2. He lays the boundaries down so there is no question where the line is between obedience and disobedience.
3. He spells out the consequences for us in advance.

Let's think about Adam and Eve in the Garden of Eden. Was God clear about what his expectations were?

First of all, he set the rule: To Adam, he said, "You are free to eat from any tree in the garden; but you must not eat from the tree of the knowledge of good and evil, for when you eat of it you will surely die" (Gen. 2:16–17).

Second, within the rule, God established the clear boundary between obedience and disobedience: "for when you eat of it..."

Third, the consequence for disobedience was clear: "you will surely die."

God's words could not have been stated more clearly: Eat from the tree in the middle of the garden and you shall surely die. As God saw Eve go to eat from the tree, he didn't say, "Now Eve, get away from that tree . . . I'm going to count to three." Equally important was his follow-through. He didn't waffle. He didn't negotiate. He followed through on the consequences that he set out in the beginning: Eat from the tree and you will surely die.

As God's child, I need to constantly remind myself to obey him *first,* and as a parent, I have an obligation to teach my children that they need to obey me the first time because God does not play the countdown to obedience game.

However, if you do not obey the LORD your God and do not carefully follow all his commands and decrees I am giving you today, all these curses will come upon you and overtake you.

DEUTERONOMY 28:15

23

DRIP, DRIP, DRIP

O ur good friend's son is playing baseball this year. Last night was baseball game number four, which was preceded by six weeks of twice weekly practices. A theme has developed: "I don't want to go to the game (or practice), Mom." The reasons are as varied as you can imagine. The coach isn't nice . . . the other kids aren't nice . . . it isn't fun . . . it's too cold . . . we're not going to win, anyway. . . ." On and on it goes, says his mom, like the dripping of a leaky faucet.

Trying to keep in mind that this is an extracurricular activity in which this child chose to take part, his parents have tried every parenting nugget in the book. They've reminded this child that he chose to play, that he's part of the team, that the team is counting on him, that it will become more fun as his—and his team's—skill improves, and most importantly, that he made the commitment and must see it through.

Still, the dripping continues. Underlying angst is heard in small murmurings and grumblings about having to go to "stupid baseball."

As I listened to this mom tell her story, she was suddenly struck by the reality of the inherent danger involved in the nagging of a dripping faucet—and her heart attitude. "Do everything without complaining or arguing" (Phil. 2:14).

She said, "To be honest, my attitude about baseball had been less than positive. I have grumbled myself about having to squeeze all of the practices and games into my schedule. I've complained about the weather, the level of play, and even the umpires. Is it any wonder my son is struggling with his attitude?"

As I listened to her bare her soul, I thought to myself, "How awesome that God knows what we need and when we need it." His specific involvement in this situation strengthened my faith. By seeing his very present work in my friend, he showed me his continued desire to work in my life too. What an awesome picture of God's amazing love for his children.

Do everything without complaining or arguing, so that you may become blameless and pure, children of God without fault in a crooked and depraved generation, in which you shine like stars in the universe.

PHILIPPIANS 2:14–15

74

24

HOW MANY HEARTS
DO YOU HAVE?

D o you remember those days on the playground when everyone of the opposite sex had cooties? I didn't hate girls, in a true sense of the word, but they just weren't cool. My buddies and I had this little game we played where we would give each other a pinch in the arm—a cootie shot—that would protect us from girl contamination just in case one of them looked at us wrong or touched our hand. Who came up with this I'll never know, but from all I hear from my three boys, this game is still alive and well on playgrounds today.

It's funny how this whole concept changes when those teen years approach. I remember one day when I was about thirteen. My grandfather was doing dishes in our kitchen. His back was turned to me when I asked him, "Pop, how many girls can I date at one time?" It was like a scene from a 1970s kung fu movie in which the little grasshopper is seeking wisdom from an old sage. Here I was, this little grasshopper, seeking wisdom from this wise older man, my grandpa.

Now my grandpa was a preacher. He loved God, and he loved God's Word. He turned slowly around, took every bit of me in, and held up one finger. "How many hearts do you have, son?" he asked.

Many years have passed since my grandpa and I had this conversation, but I've never forgotten it. I've even used his question as a counselor a couple of different times. A teenage boy I was working with was trying to date two girls at one time, and I put the question to him: "How many hearts do you have?" Just a few weeks later I was counseling the young woman whose heart he broke when he told her he no longer wanted to date her. It's a pretty powerful question.

Do you ever think God looks at your life, your choices, your thoughts, and wonders, "How many hearts do you have there, son?" I think he does this with all of us. Just think about all of the times in the Bible that we are taught about the "condition of their hearts." When God looked upon Israel and saw their unfaithfulness, he called it adultery. In Matthew 15:8–9, Jesus repeats Isaiah's prophecy of the Pharisees, "These people honor me with their lips, but their hearts are far from me. They worship me in vain; their teachings are but rules taught by men." So much of the Book of James talks about the choices we make and what God wants us to do. It states clearly that God is a jealous God—jealous for our heart's affection. "Do you think Scripture says without reason that the spirit he caused to live in us envies intensely?" (James 4:5).

How many times we try to give our heart's devotion and affection to other gods in the form of idols. An idol is anything we put in the place of God. An idol can be our dreams—passing time thinking about what we want for ourselves and our life instead of praying that God's plan for our lives would be unfolded. An idol can be our obsession with our career—we lost track of our priorities and God's will for our life in pursuit of career advancement or a bigger paycheck, forgetting that God has promised to provide for all of our needs. An idol can be in the form of a person—focusing on how to fulfill our lives through another person instead of through our relationship with God the Father.

It is easy to put things and people ahead of God in our life because he is not physically sitting, walking, living with us. Your boss is in your face, your stuff is outgrowing your house, or maybe you really need a vacation. It's easier to focus on those things because they are in your here and now. But we have been commanded to love God completely. Jesus himself stated this commandment: "Love the Lord your God with all your heart and with all your soul and with all your mind. This is the first and greatest commandment" (Matt. 22:37–38). Clearly, our first priority is to our relationship with God. No one will ever love us more, care for us more, tend to our needs in a more complete way. He is the answer we've been searching for. He longs for us to let him fill our every nook and cranny. If we keep our focus on him, he will complete us in ways we never knew possible.

Love the Lord your God with all your heart and with all your soul and with all your mind. This is the first and greatest commandment.

MATTHEW 22:37–38

25

GOOEY PANCAKE

It was a rare and wonderful treat the morning our neighbors returned from a vacation to northern Idaho and brought us a jar of fresh-picked huckleberries. These tiny little berries are about the size of a blueberry, but they are a deep, shiny purple. They grow wild in the mountains of the Northwest, and they are filled with flavor. Definitely a gift we appreciated!

My first choice when huckleberries are in the house is to make pancakes. Mmm, there is nothing like a fresh, warm huckleberry pancake. The griddle was my domain as I whipped up the batter and added a handful of the berries.

When you add a lot of berries to your pancakes, they take longer to cook. Even though they may look done, let them sit on the griddle a few extra minutes just in case. My oldest son just couldn't wait. I tried to tell him, but he kept saying, "Look at it, Dad, it's done."

This was one of those life lessons that was easier to let him learn the hard way. So I plopped the suspicious pancake on his plate, and off he went. It took only moments to hear, "Ohhh, gross!" Ah, nothing like hitting that doughy middle.

Just like my son learned that the heart of the pancake mattered, I have learned that it is my heart that really matters. Why the heart? Because everything I do or say is a reflection of my heart condition, and it is only when my heart is right with God that I will be able to walk through my day in a manner that pleases him.

Just think of all the teaching that God has given us regarding our hearts. In Exodus we read many times, "and he hardened Pharaoh's heart." God knew that to affect Pharaoh's actions he needed to go directly to his heart. In Leviticus we learn that hate is centered in our heart when God says, "Do not hate your brother in your heart" (Lev. 19:17).

In Deuteronomy we learn a wealth of knowledge about the power of our hearts. We are taught that:

- we will find God if we seek him *with all our heart* (4:29).
- we must acknowledge and *take to heart* that the Lord is God in heaven above and on the earth below; there is no other (4:39).
- we are to fear God *in our hearts* and keep his commands always, so that it might go well with us and our children forever (5:29).
- we are to love the Lord God *with all our heart* and with all our soul and with all our strength (6:5).
- the commandments he gave are to be *upon our hearts* (6:6).

Oh, the amazing potential that is in our hearts. To love, to hate, to leer, to wonder, to begrudge, to honor . . . on and on the list goes. How vital it is that God is in control of our hearts so that we honor him with our words, our choices, our very being.

May the words of my mouth and the meditation of my heart be pleasing in your sight, O Lord, my Rock and my Redeemer.

PSALM 19:14

26

FRUIT FROM
THE WOODSHED

The other night on the television, a news commentator said, "Well, he should be taken to the woodshed." You don't hear people talk about the woodshed very often. A couple days later, a friend of mine told me about her brother's wheat farm in eastern Washington state. He farms the same land that his uncle and grandfather farmed before him. The original farmhouse is still standing, with a few modernizations here and there, and many of the outbuildings are also original.

One of the unique parts of the farm is an old woodshed. These days it has been converted into a playhouse for the girls who live there, but in years gone by it served as an actual woodshed. Its purpose in those days was twofold: store wood for the cold winter months and serve as the formal woodshed of discipline. My friend's mom remembers some of the consequences she received in that old woodshed—ouch!

Pastors sometimes speak of God's woodshed—the place that God takes us when we have become spiritually disobedient. The woodshed is that place where God allows the consequences of our choices to fall into place, working his discipline in love in order to correct us.

The twelfth chapter of the Book of Hebrews talks at length about God's discipline. It states unequivocally that no one enjoys being disciplined—not the child who has made a bad choice or God's adult children who have chosen to go down a wrong path. But Hebrews also points out that the purpose of God's discipline is to teach us, to help us understand that we have made a bad choice and how to make a better choice the next time around. Discipline is not to be abusive or shaming— perhaps a good reason for the woodshed at the old farm to be used as a playhouse these days.

Disciplining my boys is one of the hardest things I do as a parent. At times I feel as if my heart is breaking as I look into one of the little guys' eyes. But I know that the greater heart-break would be not to discipline when it is merited. Proverbs instructs us to discipline our children at an early age because their hearts are tender and easier to correct. If we don't begin teaching when the children are young, their hearts can harden and the children can be set on a sinful, negative path. It really is out of love that we discipline our children. It doesn't always feel like it in the moment, but Hebrews 12:11 says, "No discipline seems pleasant at the time, but painful. Later on, however, it produces a harvest of righteousness and peace for those who have been trained by it."

God's heart aches every time we choose sin over righteousness. He grows weary from having to discipline us over and over again. But make no mistake, God disciplines those he loves just as an earthly father disciplines his son out of love. Hebrews 12:6 says that "the Lord disciplines those he loves, and he punishes everyone he accepts as a son." God's desire is that we grow more and more like him—in our words, our actions, and our thoughts. He allows us to learn from our mistakes in the great hope that we will make fewer of them in the days ahead.

A child who takes bubble gum from a store has control over his choices, but once he actually takes the gum, the consequences are out of his control. From his parents to the store owner and maybe even the police, the child's choice to take the gum without paying for it will be dealt with in an appropriate manner aimed at training and teaching. It is no different with us. We have control over the choices we make—but once we've acted, the consequences are beyond our control. God's ultimate goal is to train us, teach us, and mold us into his likeness. I must admit that I certainly hope to avoid too many visits to God's woodshed, but I know he has my best interest at heart. I look forward to the day when all of God's training will reap fields of gold. What a glorious goal!

My son, do not make light of the Lord's discipline, and do not lose heart when he rebukes you, because the Lord disciplines those he loves, and he punishes everyone he accepts as a son.

HEBREWS 12:5–6

27

THE GREAT COVER-UP

My boys are so clever. If it weren't for the crime involved in their quick action, I would have been impressed with their ability to think on their feet. But not this day.

It all started in the bathroom. I think they were out for a little harmless fun, and my wife's makeup bag looked like just the place. Unfortunately, what started out as "dress my little brother up like a clown" ended with lipstick all over the sofa. Their quick thinking came into play when they heard my footsteps coming down the hallway, looked at the mess they'd made on the cushion, and immediately flipped it over to hide their handiwork.

Of course, as we all know, this kind of quick action always comes back to haunt you. My immediate focus was on the little guy's face, but a week later when it was time to vacuum out the corners of the sofa, my attention was quickly riveted to the red marks all over the suspicious cushion.

So it is with God. Try as we might to hide our sin from him, it is always exposed. Sure, we might be able to convince ourselves that we're getting away with something in the short term, but remember how you were sure that your mother had eyes in the back of her head? Well, God doesn't need the extra set of eyes—his light reveals what is truly in our hearts.

In Ephesians 5 we are directed to "live as children of light (for the fruit of the light consists in all goodness, righteousness and truth)" (vv. 8–9). Clearly, though, God knows that we have our sin nature, because later we are reminded about the power of the light: "But everything exposed by the light becomes visible, for it is light that makes everything visible" (vv. 13–14).

Jesus himself speaks to our desire to remain in the darkness: "Light has come into the world, but men loved darkness instead of light because their deeds were evil. Everyone who does evil hates the light, and will not come into the light for fear that his deeds will be exposed" (John 3:19–20). But he goes on to say, "Whoever lives by truth comes into the light, so that it may be seen plainly that what he has done has been done through God" (v. 21).

Wow! Isn't that something? We are naturally pulled to sin, which we want to keep a secret. But when we do the right thing, we want to bask in the light because we know we couldn't have done it without God's help, and we want everyone to know it.

It just isn't a natural instinct to run and tell on ourselves. Our nature is inclined to hide when we've done wrong just as Adam and Eve tried to do in the garden and my boys tried to do with the lipstick-covered cushion. But the key is learning to be honest with God about our sinfulness and our struggles. This allows his grace to come into our lives and work miracles. Instead of flipping the cushion, we need to run to him and give it all up so he can change our hearts.

Live as children of the light . . . and find out what pleases the Lord.

EPHESIANS 5:8, 10

28

UNCONDITIONAL LOVE

It had been a rough couple of days for my oldest son. First had come his choice to act up in his kindergarten class, quickly followed by the teacher's "not pleased with your choice" response. Next had come the teacher's phone call home, followed by consequences that I think the boy knew were coming but he somehow hoped to avoid. Finally came the public apology. As part of his discipline, my son was required to apologize to his entire class, with me by his side, because what he had chosen to do had been done publicly. A lot of action for a six-year-old boy in just two days.

When I picked him up from school that day, I think he was prepared for anything, but amazingly, I was able to catch him off guard. Why? Because I took him to McDonald's for lunch—just the two of us. I explained to him that I was not taking him to McDonald's as a reward for his most recent behavior but because I loved him—unconditionally. I wanted him to know that although his behavior was wrong, I still loved him and wanted to bless him in spite of his actions in the classroom the previous day. The look on his face was priceless.

I wanted my son to know that I choose to bless him simply because he is my son. I wanted him to clearly understand that there is nothing he can do that will ever jeopardize my love for him. Yes, there are consequences for poor choices, but my love is unconditional.

How many times God has chosen to bless me in spite of me! Actually, if I stop and think about it, there probably isn't a day that goes by that God doesn't do something in my life just because he loves me. Just think about God taking on humanity simply because he loved us and did not want us to perish. "For God so loved the world that he gave his one and only Son, that whoever believes in him shall not perish but have eternal life" (John 3:16).

As if sending Christ Jesus to earth wasn't enough, God's Word tells us over and over about God's love for us. Paul tells us in the Book of Romans that there is nothing—not one single thing—that can separate us from God's love for us. "For I am convinced that neither death nor life, neither angels nor demons, neither the present nor the future, nor any powers, neither height nor depth, nor anything else in all creation, will be able to separate us from the love of God that is in Christ Jesus our Lord" (Rom. 8:38–39).

One of the great privileges of being a father is having the opportunity to teach my children about God's love for them. My unconditional love for them, blessing them in spite of their poor choices, is but a tiny picture of the amazing love God the Father has for them . . . and me!

This is love: not that we loved God, but that he loved us.

1 JOHN 4:10

29

IN THE BLINK OF AN EYE

Some friends of ours live on the West Coast. Living so close to the coast, they spend a lot of time at the Pacific Ocean, and their children have been indoctrinated on safety in and around the water. Yet it was on one of these trips to the beach that the water reached up and grabbed their youngest child. The mother shared her story with me:

> I was sitting on a very comfy, driftwood "chair" watching the three children play in the surf. They were so content and joy-filled, any cares I had were forgotten as my heart soared with theirs. Suddenly, the ocean jumped up and grabbed my youngest daughter. I ran as fast as I could, but thankfully, my son had grabbed her flailing arm just in the nick of time. All was well, if just a bit colder and wetter. My kids knew the power of the ocean—we'd been to the beach many times—but in their glee, one got a little too daring. All caution thrown to the wind in the joy of the moment. Thankfully, a stronger arm was there for the rescue.

I found myself thinking about the paradox of the ocean. It is beautiful, serene, and calming, and yet it is important not to be fooled by this wonder, for in the blink of an eye, the ocean currents can jump up and catch you, literally. This is so like life. Everything is going along so well, it is almost as if we are on a mountaintop, and then, bam, we are completely caught off guard by a storm that topples us.

When I am on a mountaintop in my life, I, just like my friend's children on the beach, can have a tendency to lose my head. Things are going along so well that I sometimes forget to check in with God, seeking his wisdom, protection, and plan. Wrapped up in my blessings, I forget whom to thank for the unbounded joy in which I am reveling. Then in the blink of an eye, a wave comes crashing to shore and carries me away. Thankfully, my all-seeing, all-knowing Father extends his hand to grab my flailing arm just in the nick of time.

Oh, thank you, God, for extending me grace day in and day out, and for faithfully rescuing me when I lose track of turning to you before I get caught by an unexpected change that rolls over me in the blink of an eye.

The eyes of the LORD are everywhere, keeping watch on the wicked and the good.

PROVERBS 15:3

30

NOT ME

Does *Not Me* live at your house? From listening to friends, loved ones, and random people I meet at the park, I think *Not Me* lives in all of our houses. Of course you know *Not Me*. He's the one who does everything.

"Who put their muddy shoes on the white couch?"
  "Not Me!"
"Who poured their peas in the toilet?"
  "Not Me!"
"Who left the dog out in the rain?"
  "Not Me!"

Ahh, if it were only as easy to find *Not Me* as it is to get to know him!

Once my boys hit that magical age when they discovered that *Not Me* lived at our house, I realized I had quite a job on my hands. In the long term, I had to help the boys understand that passing the buck to *Not Me* was a bad option. But in the short term, I had to become a detective each time there was an incident. Each time *Not Me* was named, I had to spend time and energy trying to figure out who the real culprit was.

Maybe this is why I was so touched the day my son came into the kitchen and admitted freely to his mother and me that he had just broken the blinds in the family room. I'm really not sure what instigated his confession, but I gave him mercy because I didn't have to investigate to see what had happened.

When we run to God in confession, he is anxious to forgive us. Remember, "If we confess our sins, he is faithful and just and will forgive us our sins and purify us from all unrighteousness" (1 John 1:9). God knows we are going to choose sin long before we even enter into any given situation. We cannot hide our actions or thoughts from him, so we need to do as we are taught in Hebrews: "Let us . . . approach the throne of grace with confidence, so that we may receive mercy and find grace to help us in our time of need" (Heb. 4:16).

I wish I could say that *Not Me* has been evicted from both my home and my heart, but we are all a work in progress. I find great comfort in knowing that God chose me, loves me, blesses me, and forgives me, and that through my imperfections, he is drawing my heart closer to him.

The LORD is compassionate and gracious, slow to anger, abounding in love. He will not always accuse, nor will he harbor his anger forever; he does not treat us as our sins deserve or repay us according to our iniquities.

PSALM 103:8–10

31

FRIENDSHIP

Two little girls were in the same kindergarten class. Haley and Christine had been friends since meeting at the bus stop on the first day of school. They were inseparable—until Sarah joined the class. A subtle battle was brewing between the two friends for the allegiance of this new girl. It came to a head one day just before recess.

As each child partnered with another for the walk to the playground, Haley made a beeline for Sarah. Christine was there first and asked Sarah to partner with her, but Haley grabbed Sarah's hand, saying, "She's not your friend. She's mine." The two walked off together as Christine was left standing alone. Her mother, who was helping in the classroom, could only watch as her sweet daughter grappled with what had just happened. Her instinct was to run and wrap Christine in her arms, yet she knew that on any other day, she would not have been in the classroom. Christine would need to be able to handle this situation on her own.

After a moment, Christine stood up tall, walked over to another girl who needed a partner, and asked, "Natalie, would you like to walk with me?" For the moment, all was well, but Christine's mom knew the pain of rejection that Christine experienced would revisit her as she grew through childhood and into adulthood. It is inevitable that our children will be hurt by others. Rejection is real, and rejection is painful.

As parents, one of our hardest tasks is to teach our children about friendship. We have to teach them what true friendship looks like. True friends accept you for who you are, and they make you feel good when you are around them. They are not constantly critical, and they do not try to make themselves feel better by tearing you down. True friends are unselfish, thinking of the other person instead of just themselves or their own needs. A true friend is loyal—no matter the cost.

Our greatest example of a true friend is Jesus. He is forever loyal—always there for us no matter where we've been. He is, as Proverbs 18:24 describes, the kind of friend who sticks closer than a brother. Isn't that amazing? Jesus will be there for us day or night, in good times and in bad. He will never leave or abandon us—what an amazing example for us.

A man of many companions may come to ruin, but there is a friend who sticks closer than a brother.

PROVERBS 18:24

32

TELLING THE EMPEROR THE TRUTH

The emperor has no clothes. Do you remember this story? In a nutshell, the emperor loved new clothes—they were his passion. He spent all his money on beautiful clothes. One day two swindlers came to town claiming they were weavers who could make the finest cloth imaginable. Not only were the colors and patterns extraordinarily beautiful, but the material had an amazing property that made it invisible to anyone who was incompetent or stupid. The emperor immediately gave them gold and fine silk to weave their cloth for him.

When the swindlers presented the new clothes to the emperor, none of his ministers, attendants, nor the emperor himself would admit they could not see the clothes, because that would mean they were incompetent or stupid. Completely enamored with himself, the emperor wanted to parade his beautiful new clothes before the townspeople. A majestic parade was held, and it was a great event. The music began, and down the street paraded the emperor—in his nakedness. The people applauded and cheered for the emperor, shouting, "Look at his new clothes!" Everyone could see that he was naked, but not one single adult had the courage to say it. They merely chose the easy path—to play along with the charade. It took a child to call attention to the truth, "The emperor has no clothes!"

This is one of the guarantees with young children—they will tell the naked truth. If Grandma has no teeth, it's a guarantee that you will hear, "Look, Mommy, Grandma doesn't have any teeth!" If Grandpa doesn't have a single hair on his head, little Susie will announce it to anyone within earshot. It's one of the gifts of childhood—telling things exactly the way they appear.

Not telling what we see is a skill we learn as we mature, and I use the word *skill* loosely. Recently, I was reading about a prominent basketball coach. It seems he has built quite a reputation for his temper—unleashing angry tirades on the sidelines, throwing profanity around with ease, and tossing a few chairs to boot—yet people consistently praise him. They talk about what an intellectual he is, how he's able to converse on any topic, and what a gifted motivator he is. The funny—not funny ha-ha but funny perplexing—thing is that this successful basketball coach has never taken responsibility for his behavior. For any given temper tantrum there is someone or something else to blame. And the subject is off-limits. No one dare confront this man lest he be labeled a betrayer. Quite a story.

One of the most distinguishing marks of maturity is the ability to admit our shortcomings. When we have "no clothes on," we need to be able to admit it—without resorting to playing games of denial or blame. Someone has taken the word *denial* and formed an acrostic that says, "Don't even know I am lying to myself." If we want to live a life that honors God, it is essential to see the truth for what it really is.

Proverbs 27:6 (NASB) says, "Faithful are the wounds of a friend, but deceitful are the kisses of an enemy." Hearing the naked truth can be hard for anyone, but a lie distorts and perverts. We need to deal with our inner enemy—that little voice inside of us that wants to pretend we're really not naked—and we desperately need to welcome the voices of people who speak the truth to us in love and say, "The emperor has no clothes."

It might sound like this: "Johnny, in the way you're relating to your wife and your children, you're naked and you have no clothes on. You're wrong." Or, "Michelle, in the way you unleash your anger toward others, you're naked and you're wrong." Or, "Sir or Ma'am, in the way you're handling the finances, cooking the firm's books, you're naked and lacking in integrity."

It's important to remember our "truth circle" can say the words, but it is up to us to listen and respond. Proverbs says that a wise person hears and receives instruction and profits by it, but a foolish person stiffens his neck; he doesn't hear it. Let's live our lives in reality, being willing and eager to grow up in our character and grow deeper in our integrity. Let's be willing to clothe ourselves in humility, compassion, and true godly character.

Listen to advice and accept instruction, and in the end you will be wise.

PROVERBS 19:20

33

TONGUE FU

Each night around the dinner table, my children, my wife, and I share about our day. A few weeks ago, as the kids were taking their turns, I noticed that their comments weren't so much about *what* as about *who*. One started out, "We went to art and Matthew..." Another added, "Oh, the last time we were in art, Taylor..." I was intrigued by this conversation pattern, because it is one that is entirely normal and modeled by grown-ups everywhere.

Being completely honest here, it is just flat out easier to talk about some*one* than some*thing*. Even when we don't intend to do this, it happens. Just like the kids, we start out talking about something that happened (art class), but we easily flow into talking about the someone who was involved (Taylor or Matthew).

There's a word for this type of conversation: gossip. Idle chatter about a person other than ourselves is dangerous. My tongue can cause so much trouble if I don't monitor it carefully, and apparently, I need to do a better job of teaching my children about this wily character.

This is hard! Walking what is sometimes a very fine line between general sharing and gossip is a challenge for many of us—much less for three children under the age of ten. What I've tried to clarify for the kids is that they are like a reporter. They get to share about their day in a "just the facts, ma'am" kind of way. Back to the art class, we really only need to know what Matthew did if it affected Jordan in a personal way. Even then, the focus is on what happened to Jordan, not on disparaging Matthew.

In David McCullough's book *John Adams,* a great lesson is shared of Abigail Smith Adams's father, the Reverend Smith. "They must never speak unkindly of anyone, Abigail remembered her father saying repeatedly. They must say only 'handsome things,' and make topics rather than persons their subjects." What a great life principle for us all to follow. Learning the art of conversation is hard work but well worth the time and effort. Topics—not persons. What a great place to start.

Do not let any unwholesome talk come out of your mouths, but only what is helpful for building others up according to their needs, that it may benefit those who listen.

EPHESIANS 4:29

97

34

STICKS AND STONES

Sticks and stones will break my bones,
but words will never hurt me.

I heard it so many times as a child that I could never forget it, but this axiom was brought fresh to mind one day last fall. It was as if the wounds of my kindergarten year had been slashed open again—and this is not a good thing. It was one of the first days of kindergarten for my son, and I was helping in the classroom. The children really didn't know one another yet, and they were all wearing name tags. The cutest little girl walked up to another child and said, "Hi, Sammy. I'm Katie." He turned to her, looked her up and down, and said, "Don't talk to me, you fat pig." It was gut-wrenching.

Sammy seemed like a timid little kid, and maybe his words flowed from his fear, but they were cutting. Katie recovered pretty well, saying, "Well, Sammy, I'm taller than you."

Sammy, not to be outdone, retorted, "Well, my brother Michael is taller than you." Katie gave up, and Sammy looked satisfied. I sat in absolute wonderment, thankful in that small moment that the teacher got to handle this one.

It isn't just the very young who throw words around that brand like fire. A fifth grader told me that kids in his class didn't like him. I was a bit taken aback because he's a good kid, works hard, etc. So, I said, "I can't believe it. Sure they do."

He replied, "Well, I went up to this girl named Michelle and I said, 'Michelle, are you my friend?' And Michelle said, 'No, I'm not your friend, and I never want to be your friend.'"

Yikes! I felt so badly for this boy. He's a tenderhearted kid who just wants to be accepted and liked. Can you imagine putting yourself out there in the way he did?

Words are amazingly powerful. They can build you up as high as Mount Everest but just as quickly rip your guts out. There is no question that, as fun and as enjoyable as children can be, they can also be brutal toward one another. Unfortunately, children have to be taught about the power of their words—or they can grow into adults who also underestimate the power of the firebrand in their mouth.

Reliving the kindergarten nightmare, I wanted to give my boys a picture of what happens when words fly out of your mouth. So on one of our family nights, we took a tube of toothpaste, spread it all over some newspaper on the floor, and told the boys that we would give them five dollars if they could figure out a way to get the toothpaste off the floor and back into the tube—as neatly as possible, of course.

I'm not sure if it was their eagerness to get the money or their confidence in the task at hand, but they actually tried to put the toothpaste back in that tube. Within about a minute, they said, "Dad, this is hard. We can't figure out a way to do it." I agreed— there really is no way to accomplish this task, trust me—and then I tried to draw them a picture.

I said, "Guys, when you call each other names, when you call each other 'pickle brain' or 'mushroom lips' or 'marshmallow nose' or 'chicken,' those names and words are out there—you can't take them back—just like the toothpaste. These words are not wholesome, and they can cause a lot of hurt and maybe even anger and resentment." I think the boys are starting to get the message. We are a work in progress, but I have seen some positive change.

The tongue is a wily little creature that will wreak havoc if we let it. We have to make a conscious effort to rein it in—and it is only possible with God's intervention. The Book of James has wonderful direction on the power of the tongue. It says, "No man can tame the tongue. It is a restless evil, full of deadly poison" (James 3:8). My Bible is so marked up in James that I can scarcely read it anymore—I am a work in progress.

Our tongue can be either a butcher knife, cutting into someone's self-esteem, or it can be a butter knife, spreading positive words. Ephesians 4:29 tells us that we are to let no unwholesome words come out of our mouths but only words that build up people. So we have a choice to make. We can either commit to the way of tongue fu, letting our tongue run as it pleases, or we can choose to speak tender words, words seasoned with salt, words that build others up, encourage, and affirm.

Whoever said, "Sticks and stones will break my bones, but words will never hurt me," was not telling the truth. Words do harm, so let us choose to speak words of love today.

The tongue has the power of life and death, and those who love it will eat its fruit.

PROVERBS 18:21

35

JUST KIDDING

Did you ever play what you thought was a funny, practical joke on your mother, only to find that she really didn't think it was very funny at all? At a couples' dinner the other night, a friend shared that she pulled the ultimate no-no on her mom.

> I remember the look on my mother's face as if it were yesterday. My brother and I were playing outside. Somehow, I thought it would be really funny to yell, "Mom, come quick, Tom's been hit by a car!" Funny was the last word that could have applied. I tried to tell her that I was just kidding, but the effect was not good.
>
> A few months later, the brick wall that held the railing on our front porch fell on my brother's leg while he was pulling on the railing. When I went yelling for my mom, her response was lackadaisical because of that prank about the car. The problem was that this time it was real. Lesson learned!

We can probably all agree that there is nothing funny about sending your mother's heart rate to the moon and back in a matter of moments, but sometimes the "I was just kidding" issues are a bit more gray. As parents, we really can't tell if the joke was meant to be funny or hurtful.

Consider a boy who has all the makings of growing into a towering, lithe NBA star. While this might mean all kinds of great things for his future as a basketball player, there could be some question about the intent of a sibling's comment, "Your feet look like sleds—oops, I was just kidding!"

Our family has a phenomenal collection of photo albums, thanks to the dedication and hard work of my wife. My youngest child loves to look at them time and time again. He is a naturally funny little guy, and so many of the photos of him as a baby are just funny. When one of his brothers said, "You are just goofy. Look at all these pictures!" he said he was just kidding, But was he?

Sometimes people really are just kidding, but sometimes I think we use the "just kidding" phrase as a cop-out to mask our anger or frustration. Proverbs 26:18–19 says, "Like a madman shooting firebrands or deadly arrows is a man who deceives his neighbor and says, 'I was only joking!'" Wow, that is an incredible word picture. The author of Proverbs is telling us that deception is deception—even when we say we're just kidding. We can say we are only joking, but in our heart there may be churning firebrands or deadly arrows.

What we struggle to interpret as parents, God knows for certain because he knows the intent of our hearts. Perhaps we are warned to avoid this pattern of deceit because our words are a reflection of our heart, and God knows that if there is angst in our heart, it will come flying out our mouth. We can easily fall into this pattern in comfortable relationships, like marriage. A buddy of mine has been married quite a long time, but he and his wife have never resolved the issue of clutter in their house. He would like there to be none—she is looking for a little more balance but tries diligently to keep things in order. It seems resolved, until a stray pair of shoes litters the entryway or books are scattered across a corner of the family room. "I know I should just pick the shoes up and move on, but I make the comment, 'I was carrying this box up the stairs . . . thank goodness I didn't trip on your shoes . . . ha, ha!' It's not funny, but it is a clear picture of my heart attitude." My friend knows he needs to rid his heart of this issue because the cutting, subtle comments aren't a bit healthy for him, his wife, or his marriage. Our words are a picture of our heart attitude, and God knows our heart.

It is *so* easy to fall into this habit. Listen carefully to your children—and then to yourself. Take extra care to have the words of your heart flow out of your mouth in a way that honors God.

The lips of the righteous nourish many, but fools die for lack of judgment.

PROVERBS 10:21

36

NOTHING BUT THE TRUTH

There is one harsh reality I've learned well as a parent—kids are brutally honest whether you want them to be or not! If the truth be told, young children often voice what we are thinking—but would never say. Kids are known to say things like, "Daddy, her breath smells funny!" Okay, be honest now, weren't you thinking it? They say, "Daddy, your belly's really big!" Hmm, of course none of you were thinking that! Embarrassed or not, we parents should be applauding our children's unique nature to tell the truth. Yes, there is a degree of tact that we need to teach, but the day is coming when truth will begin to blur for them just as it has for many of us.

Too often, when someone asks us what we think about such and such, we tend to say what we think the other person wants to hear, couching the truth to protect feelings or to be politically correct. Oh, the benefit of being truthful. Proverbs says, "The Lord detests lying lips, but he delights in men who are truthful" (Prov. 12:22). God wants us to be considerate of the feelings of others but not at the cost of lying.

Our culture is awash in deceit. It is everywhere around us, largely because people don't want to be seen as offensive or controversial. Even in the church, this is running rampant. Christians are afraid to speak the truth for fear of being ridiculed or seen as intolerant or judgmental. Recently, a buddy of mine was telling me about a man he'd met at his monthly men's breakfast:

> He was a fresh, new Christian and had experienced what I would call a modern-day version of Paul's amazing conversion on the road to Damascus. He told me that he had long attended another church in the area. One morning, a few months prior, he had announced to his table at a men's event that he was going to divorce his wife. Tears formed in his eyes as he recounted the experience of not one man approaching him with God's wisdom about divorce. Rather, they consoled him about his hard luck, one even offering to introduce him to the singles' pastor. In his new walk with God, his heart was breaking for the sinful path he almost turned down—and not even Christians were willing to speak the truth in love.

Our goal in parenting is to take our children's gift for truth-telling and help them combine it with love. As we are teaching this great lesson to our children, we may need to relearn it ourselves. Ephesians 4:15 tells us that we ought to speak the truth in love. It is a trait we must master to live the life God calls us to. Remember, truth without love is brutal—but love without truth isn't really love at all.

Speaking the truth in love, we will in all things grow up into him who is the Head, that is, Christ.

EPHESIANS 4:15

37

FINDING STRENGTH THROUGH WEAKNESS

When my first son was born, I marveled at his perfection. I remember thinking, "Don't worry, little guy, I'm your daddy. I will keep you safe, protected, and loved."

In those early years, keeping this pledge was relatively easy. If he was wet, I would change his diaper. If he was hungry, I would feed him. My wife and I made sure his crib was safe, that he slept in the "right" position, and that he was warm, cuddled, and secure. As he grew, keeping Little Johnny Austin safe and protected was mostly about securing his environment and just being there, ever vigilant. I'm sure you remember those days—gates on the stairs, covers on the outlets, and an always present, watchful eye. The hurts of a curious toddler were eased by a kiss, a Band-Aid, and a hug.

The pains of a growing boy are not so easily soothed. The soul-ache of rejection and just plain meanness is much harder to fix than the scuff of a knee. And to be honest, I have found that the dad in me wants to do just that—fix the situations my son is facing to protect him from having to experience the pains of growing up.

My son is naturally gregarious, making friends easily wherever he goes. Because of this, I really didn't think too much as he began his second year at a new school. Much to my surprise, however, this transition has been anything but seamless. Changing schools has been a difficult transition for him. He has been faced with a level of unfriendliness that is foreign to him, and he has found himself the scapegoat in a number of precarious situations. Finding his place in this new world has not been easy.

The other night at bedtime, the depth of Johnny Austin's pain became clear to me when he asked if he could just go back to his old school. I knew he had been having a tough time, but in that moment, when it was just the two of us, my heart ached for him so deeply. I felt his pain and wanted to march over to that school the next morning and have a few words with his classmates!

As I sought God's direction in how to parent this situation, I realized that being Dad-the-Bully wasn't the answer. I heard God very clearly guide me: "Johnny, don't protect him from this pain. Join him there, be present in the pain with him, and help him walk through it so he learns how to deal with conflict, how to be assertive, and how to set boundaries. My grace is sufficient for Johnny Austin just as it is for you."

In Psalm 3, David cries out to God amid great trial. "O LORD, how many are my foes! How many rise up against me!" (v. 1). "But you are a shield around me, O LORD; you bestow glory on me and lift up my head. To the LORD I cry aloud, and he answers me from his holy hill" (vv. 3–4). Two things were very clear to me. First, trials are a part of the life that we are called to live; and second, God is always in our corner, ready to answer me from his holy hill.

Again in the Twenty-third Psalm, we are reminded that God is always present, wanting to provide us comfort and strength in our times of trial. "The LORD is my shepherd, I shall not be in want. . . . Even though I walk through the valley of the shadow of death, I will fear no evil, for you are with me; your rod and your staff, they comfort me" (vv. 1, 4).

107

In my soul-searching, I found myself thinking of the apostle Paul. In 2 Corinthians he cries out to God to remove the thorn from his side: "Three times I pleaded with the Lord to take it away from me. But he said to me, 'My grace is sufficient for you, for my power is made perfect in weakness.' Therefore I will boast all the more gladly about my weaknesses, so that Christ's power may rest on me" (12:8–9).

That was God's message to me. The way I wanted to protect my son was exactly how God wants to protect you and me when he sees the enemy toying with us. God, through Christ Jesus, wants to shield us, to protect us, to shower love upon us. But God never promises to keep us from pain. He joins with us. He is Immanuel, the ever-present God. He feels our agony and our pain deeply. He sent the Spirit to walk with us through these trying times, but he doesn't take the pain or the rejection away. He uses it to strengthen us, because in our weakness we become strong in him, just as Paul did.

I still want to take my son's pain away. It is amazing to me how much his emotional aches tear at the deepest reaches of my heart. But knowing that God, the Father, feels exactly the same way helps comfort me. To know too that there is much to be gained by the trial-laden path each of my sons will walk in this life brings me comfort, because their emotional struggles are not in vain. They serve a great purpose, drawing them closer to God, their heavenly Father. He is all they need.

My grace is sufficient for you, for my power is made perfect in weakness.

2 CORINTHIANS 12:9

38

GARLIC WATER,
ANYONE?

Thirsts. Everyone has them. Think back to the long, hot, dog days of last summer when you might have spent a couple of hours in the outdoors. A cool drink certainly hits the spot in times like that.

When we are thirsty, our craving for a drink is more obvious and immediate to us than the covert thirsts of our soul that yearn to express themselves and that we—to our shame—often defer addressing. As a child, I spent much time at my grand-parents' house. My grandma had a thirst for garlic water, espe-cially during the summertime. I loved Grandma dearly, but how could anyone develop a taste for garlic water? She downed that stuff as though it were Kool-Aid.

On one particularly hot, sticky summer day, after hours of serious playing, I was thirsty—really thirsty, one of those deep down body thirsts. To Grandma I headed, a familiar pattern by then. I went bursting into her kitchen and swung the refriger-ator door wide open, trusting that I would find a delicious, cool quencher for my thirst. I spotted one that looked inviting. It was full to the brim, a nice brown color, and looked like it was saying, "Drink me, Johnny, drink me!"

Grandma had two simple rules for her young grandchildren. One, you were not to go into the refrigerator and get a drink without first asking her. Two, you were to get a cup and pour a drink rather than drink directly from the pitcher. Whoever said confession is good for the soul was probably never as thirsty as I was at that moment. Nonetheless, I confess some thirty years later that I violated both rules.

As I recall, there were two pitchers of drink in the fridge that day. Can you guess which pitcher I eagerly raised to my little parched lips? Gulp, gulp, gulp, gulp. Yuck! Garlic water! There was neither label nor warning of what was inside those pitchers. Too late it occurred to me that there was only one person who knew for sure—Grandma. If I had only consulted her, she would have led me to a satisfying and enjoyable drink.

One of the first Scripture verses I began memorizing after I became a Christian was Proverbs 3:5–6 (KJV): "Trust in the LORD with all thine heart; and lean not unto thine own understanding. In all thy ways acknowledge him, and he shall direct thy paths." Just like Grandma, my wife and I require our boys to inquire of us before getting something out of the refrigerator. Their thirst and cravings are valid, but in there are items too heavy for them to handle and things that can create a real mess if spilled. Is our heavenly Father any different in his loving requirements of us? Yes, we have legitimate thirsts and appetites. That is how we were made. What gets us off track is when we seek to meet those legitimate thirsts in illegitimate ways. This is what the Bible calls sin.

Adam and Eve needed to eat, but they were clearly told not to go near the Tree of the Knowledge of Good and Evil. Our deepest thirst is for intimacy. God is the Father of intimacy and longs for us to experience rich, authentic intimacy. Do we make it a point to consult with our Father about our desires and decisions, or do we simply end up drinking garlic water? That is the fruit of trying to get our legitimate needs met in illegitimate ways. The Father wants to be consulted. He knows our need for attention has significance. When we do not consult the Father, we wind up pursuing our own lusts. Lust is when we become consumed and pursue something apart from God—when we end up pursuing garlic water intimacy in the form of food, unhealthy relationships, and debilitating addictions of all kinds. Whatever we pursue as a thirst quencher apart from the God who is the Source of living water becomes merely a mirage in the desert of a parched soul.

God placed a thirst inside Abraham and Sarah for a son. He told them he would satisfy their desires for a male child, but in his time. His time took about twenty-five years. During those long, hot years, Abraham and Sarah stood at the door of Sarah's womb waiting for God to come and open it up. But, like us, they grew impatient, so much so that they began to play "Let's Make a Deal."

They chose door number two and concocted their own drink, called Hagar. Sarah influenced her husband to think that per-haps God would use Hagar, their servant girl, to bring them their son through her womb. There is no indication that Abra-ham objected to having relations with the youthful, no doubt vivacious, Hagar—with his wife's permission, of course. At the time, the idea seemed brilliant and tasted great to their senses. It proved to be less filling in the long run, however.

God desires that we experience Isaacs in our lives and min-istries. Isaac was God's intended blessing—a reward for faith-fulness. The name Isaac is from the Hebrew word for laughter. When the Angel of the Lord told Abraham that Sarah would have a child in her old age, Sarah laughed incredulously. After all these years, after hope against hope, after all the ridicule from her servant, Hagar—Sarah would have her own child.

God does not want us to settle for Ishmaels, which is what we experience when we choose something other than what God intends for us. God says in effect, I want to cultivate within you a spring of living water that will be the thirst quencher of your soul. The world and the enemy will offer you sour, bitter-tast-ing cups from which to drink. I want to offer you a better cup. When you have a day of relationship challenges and intense spiritual warfare, come near my fountain, and drink deeply of my refreshing water of life and strength. I do not want you to imbibe garlic water. I want you to pursue and consult with me, and drink with me. As a father, I do know best.

Everyone who drinks this water will be thirsty again, but whoever drinks the water I give him will never thirst. Indeed, the water I give him will become in him a spring of water welling up to eternal life.

JOHN 4:13–14

39

BUILDING ON
THE RIGHT STUFF

I'm pretty sure that when I was the child, sitting in my mother's lap as she read me fairy tale after fairy tale, I didn't see the life lessons as clearly as I do now that I'm the parent. But these witty little stories are full of great stuff.

My youngest son's current favorite is *The Tale of the Three Little Pigs,* and though I would like to think it's the moral of the story that grabs him, I'm pretty sure it's the huffing and the puffing! On first read, it's easy to think that *The Tale of the Three Little Pigs* is just a cute little vignette about two not-so-bright pigs, a loud, windy wolf, and one pig that has more on the ball than the others. But, in reality, this story is really about facing adversity and the importance of what we build our house on.

In the story, each of the three pigs faced adversity as they went out into the world to build their houses. The first little pig, as you recall, built with hay and straw. He faced adversity when the big bad wolf came knocking, eventually huffing and puffing until the little pig's house blew down. His house demolished, the little pig ran right to his brother's house, which the brother had built with wood. That house, too, was demolished when the big bad wolf huffed and puffed and blew it down. Thankfully for the pigs, their third brother was a little bit more forward thinking. As they ran to his house, they saw that he had built with bricks. The big bad wolf arrived on the scene, but his huffing and puffing was no match for the little brick house. He blew and blew, but it was futile. The house, built on a firm foundation, withstood this storm of adversity.

Adversity will come to our lives. It may not visit us today or tomorrow, but we can know with certainty that our times of trial are just down the road. It might be in the form of an enemy who wants to huff and puff until he blows our lives away. Or maybe it will hit us in the circumstances of life—we lose our job or have a major illness that finds us with more month than money. Death, loneliness, career challenges, sickness, disease—adversity will affect and impact every single one of us. We are not immune from the trials of life, so the real question is what have we built our houses—our lives—on?

Just as it was with the pigs, what we choose as our foundation is critical to our weathering the storms that will come. What we choose to build our house with will determine whether we are blown over or left standing, our feet firmly planted.

In Matthew 7 Jesus talks about two kinds of builders. He says, "Everyone who hears these words of mine and puts them into practice is like a wise man who built his house on the rock. The rain came down, the streams rose, and the winds blew and beat against that house; yet it did not fall, because it had its foundation on the rock. But everyone who hears these words of mine and does not put them into practice is like a foolish man who built his house on sand. The rain came down, the streams rose, and the winds blew and beat against that house, and it fell with a great crash" (vv. 24–27). Jesus called the person who built his life on sand a foolish person and the one who built on rock a wise builder. Both these builders were faced with adversity— the storms came—but only one was left standing.

We are all going to face adversity. The key is to make sure that our foundation is built on God's Word. If we build our lives according to his blueprints, no matter the depth and breadth of our trials, our house, our very life, will withstand the storms of life.

Unless the Lord builds the house, its builders labor in vain.

PSALM 127:1

114

40

WATCH YOUR STEP

L egos are going to be the death of me. Don't get me wrong. I love what my boys can build with Legos. I appreciate the way these little building blocks challenge their thinking process. But if I step on one more hard, pointy piece of plastic in the middle of the night as I'm trying to navigate down the hallway toward the bathroom . . . well, you get the picture.

This clutter is one of the many realities of having children in our homes. Yes, we can have a place for every little piece of every little toy, but somehow there are still random traps left lying about. These toys are like booby traps—I never know where they will turn up until it's too late. As silly as it may sound, I've actually thought about carrying a flashlight with me so I can make these midnight trips safely.

When I come in contact with one of these innocent traps, my reaction is swift. I grab my aching toe or heel to massage away the pain. As the physical pain begins to subside, I am left with an *ugh* feeling in my heart. The *ugh* is a combination of frustration and anger I feel toward my boys for leaving the toys scattered about in the first place. I work through these mini-moments of *ugh*, and I'm confident that we're making progress on having a place for everything and everything in its place. In the meantime, I've found myself thinking about the booby traps of life.

Far more damaging than the Lego booby trap in my dark hallway are the booby traps that await you and me as we walk through each of our days. From driving on the freeway to navigating the parking lot at a local shopping mall, from a conversation with our boss to practicing conflict resolution with our spouse, the opportunities for us, as Christians, to get snared by a booby trap are countless. Some, like the Legos, are created innocently by others, and we inadvertently stumble in simply because we aren't paying enough attention to what we are doing. Others, like driving ten miles over the speed limit down the freeway, are choices we make because—well, just because. Other traps are laid out by the sin of others, and then we have to choose whether to willingly participate in the sin or to take a stand for righteousness.

Just the other day, a friend of mine found herself in potential booby trap territory. Part of her daily routine is to drive her children to and from school. On this particular day, she arrived a few minutes early and found a group of parents gathered in the foyer. They were also waiting for their children, but to pass the time, they were engaged in a hot conversation about one of the teachers. Coincidentally, my friend's daughter was in the classroom of the teacher being disparaged.

The easiest option for my friend would have been to just keep walking. It wasn't her conversation, and it didn't have to be her battle. Yet this teacher had given her heart and soul to my friend's daughter all year long. Sure, there had been a few bumps along the road, but all in all, it had been a good year. Hmm, take the easy way out or do the right thing. Booby trap!

My friend had to choose. The easy way would be safe and free from the risk of ridicule or scorn, but at what cost? Ridicule or scorn from her peers or the consequences of choosing a path that was not consistent with God's direction? She chose to speak up because she feared God's disappointment far more than that of the women in the foyer. The great thing was that God protected her. As she spoke up, another woman who had been silent joined in the conversation, sharing that she, too, admired this teacher because of her commitment to her son. God honored my friend's right choice.

The path that will keep us from falling headfirst into a booby trap is not always so well marked. Often we are literally grappling around in the dark, trying to find our way. In these situations (and all others, too) we need to remember that God is with us. He knows where the traps are, and he wants to be our flashlight, guiding us through those dark passages. If we seek God's direction, he will not let us fall.

Throughout Psalm 37 we are reminded to seek the Lord and to commit our way to him. In the moments when I am most likely to fall prey to a booby trap, I remember verses 23 and 24 of this great psalm:

If the LORD delights in a man's way, he makes his steps firm; though he stumble, he will not fall, for the LORD upholds him with his hand.

PSALM 37:23–24

117

41

VOICE OF LOVE

The thought of losing one of my boys had never occurred to me. I remember listening to a friend talk about it one day. She had lost track of one of her children earlier in the week at a local Easter egg hunt, and it reminded her of a day long ago when she had been the lost child instead of the grown-up.

Growing up, I had the tendency to wander. It wasn't an intentional thing, but I was so intrigued by the people around me, I would stop to talk to them, completely oblivious to where my mom was headed. I remember one time when my mom and I were in a department store. She had been right next to me when I got involved in a conversation with someone. (Remember, this was quite a few years ago when the world was a different place.) Suddenly I looked around and realized I was utterly alone. I couldn't see my mom anywhere. It didn't really startle me. I just walked to the customer service gal, who announced over the microphone, "Would the mother of . . . please come to Customer Service." My mom came running in a state of frightened panic. To me, it wasn't really that big of a deal, but she was frantic. It's funny how a few years can completely change your perspective. Now that

I'm the parent, I so fully understand why my mom reacted the way she did. There are few things more frightening than to be in a crowded area of people and to lose your child.

Listening to her story, I remember thinking, "Funny . . . interesting . . . but I just can't relate." Then it happened to me. We were at the mall. One minute my son was right next to me, and the next minute, I couldn't see him anywhere. Not having access to a loudspeaker, I simply began to call out for him. "Johnny, Johnny, Johnny . . ." The area was crowded with people, but my son heard me and knew my voice. We couldn't see each other, but he kept walking toward the direction from which he heard my voice coming. We found each other in a matter of moments, though it seemed much longer at the time.

God calls for us in this same way. He longs for us to be walking right alongside him. When we separate ourselves from him, his loving voice beckons us to return. He seeks us, calling over and over again for us to come back to him. He says,

My sheep listen to my voice; I know them, and they follow me.

JOHN 10:27

42

TRUST ME

Someday each of my boys is going to look me in the eye and say, "I'm not so sure about this, Dad, but I trust you, so let's go." But this was not going to be that day.

We were at an amusement park, and we had spent most of our time riding two of the rides in the children's area. Now don't get me wrong, these rides were fine, but I knew there were many more down the road, just waiting for us to come and find them. When I mentioned heading on, you would have thought I proposed getting shots at the doctor's office. The boys cried, bucked me, and resisted me. I had nothing but good planned for them, yet they didn't trust me. To be brutally honest, I was hurt that they didn't trust me.

In the end, I almost literally had to carry them to the other part of the park. It was painful for me—and for them. Once we got there, the boys were ecstatic. Our day was not ruined by this momentary difference of opinion, but it did leave me wondering what God must think when we resist him.

I am awestruck by the wall of faith God has built. Time and time again, throughout the Bible, we are reminded of the great things God has done—promises he has made and fulfilled.

Do you remember in Genesis when God commanded Noah to build the ark? He said, "I am going to put an end to all people, for the earth is filled with violence because of them. . . . So make yourself an ark" (Gen. 6:13–14). God gave Noah very specific instructions on how to build the ark, and then he made a covenant with Noah. He said, "I am going to bring floodwaters on the earth to destroy all life. . . . But I will establish my covenant with you, and you will enter the ark—you and your sons and your wife and your sons' wives with you" (Gen. 6:17–18). Then, the most amazing part of this passage, "Noah did everything just as God commanded him" (Gen. 6:22). Isn't that incredible? When I think of all the things that might have been running through Noah's head—"Wait, but what about . . ."—he obeyed. He trusted God to lead him, to protect him, to walk with him down the path that God had specifically designed for him.

The Bible is filled with stories like this—examples of God's faithfulness—and yet we fail to trust him. My own life is filled with times when God has been there for me. If I had placed a stone in my backyard every time God helped me, I would have a wall that reaches to the sky. Yet I question him at times. I think, "Oh, I can just do this one thing because God really doesn't have a plan for the here and now." How wrong I am. There are few things as certain as the simple fact that God is trustworthy. He is a covenant-making God, and he wants us to trust his heart of goodness. He is waiting for the day I look up to him and say, "I'm not so sure about this, Dad, but I trust you, so let's go."

Trust in the LORD with all your heart and lean not on your own understanding; in all your ways acknowledge him, and he will make your paths straight.

PROVERBS 3:5–6

43

LIVING WATER

The daughter of a friend was agonizing over her sick child. She had a high fever and had been vomiting for several days. She was vomiting almost every hour for the first day, and if she tried to drink anything, it would come right back up. The child was desperately thirsty and in a feverish delirium. She begged for water, which, of course, her mother couldn't allow her to have (not to mention not being able to give her the medicine that would bring down her fever). Finally, in the right time, her mother was able to give the child small sips, but it was a long walk of drought as the child pleaded for a truly life-giving fluid.

As I watched my friend walk through this desert with her daughter, I found myself deeply in awe of our Lord. He drew the most amazing picture for me. A child, sick with fever, desperate for comfort and relief, cared for by a mother who loved the child so deeply she would do almost anything for her. Yet the one thing the child wanted—water—the mother could not give. The child didn't understand, and the mother, her heart breaking, did the only thing she knew to do. Hold the child, comfort the child, reassure the child that the sickness—her time in the desert—would pass.

Have you been in the desert? Maybe your marriage is a dry and weary place. Perhaps it is one of your children who has drawn you to the parched land. Maybe you've simply lost God somewhere, leaving you desperately thirsty but not sure how to find relief.

Just as my friend provided comfort to her daughter, so God provides comfort to you. It is hard to sense him sometimes. I know I've found myself thinking, "Where are you, God? How can you leave me out here by myself?" But God is there—always and forever, holding us up as we cross our desert. We don't even realize his steady hands are holding us up, often because we are so focused on the pain of our journey that we don't stop to think about all he promises us.

I didn't understand why my friend's little girl had to get so sick. On the surface, it seemed silly and senseless for her to have to go through that terrible time. Yet it strengthened her. Her body will be more able to fight off a similar virus should it come around again. Her relationship with her mother grew stronger as they spent those many hours together. She learned in a deeper way that she could trust her mother to do the right thing—even when it hurt.

When I have been in the desert, I have rarely seen a reason for it until much later. In the middle of the trial, it seems silly and senseless. Yet once I am beyond the dry time, God allows me to see clearly the *whys* and *hows* of my time in the desert. There are always lessons learned, strength built, perseverance increased. That amazing parallel again between a loving mother for her child and my heavenly Father for me: I can always trust him to do the right thing—even when it hurts.

In God's time, he will provide us the life-giving drink for which we so desperately yearn.

Sometimes we ask God for things that we *know* are good, but he says, "No" or "Not at this time." We can't understand why, so we beg, plead, and bargain. Yet God doesn't provide until we are ready, and even then it is often only in small sips. Truly, I sometimes cannot see why God withholds the water of life, but I do know and believe that his plan is bigger than my vision, even when it involves deep distress and pain.

O God, you are my God, earnestly I seek you; my soul thirsts for you, my body longs for you, in a dry and weary land where there is no water.

PSALM 63:1

123

44

DADDY, WHATCHA' DOIN'?

Engrossed in my morning routine, I hadn't heard my young son enter the bathroom. When he piped up with, "Daddy, whatcha' doin'?" I almost shaved off my left eyebrow. Luckily, I recovered before losing the brow and proceeded to have a mind-boggling conversation about the *hows* and *whys* of shaving that one can only have with a three-year-old.

Have you ever noticed how the conversations you have with children—especially very young ones—are filled with, "Okay, but why?" There never seems to be enough information to satisfy the curious minds of the young. That morning, my son accepted as reality that I shave hair from my face every day—but why? It made sense to him that the electric razor I use was part of the process—but why? As a matter of fact, why did I have to do this in the first place? Whiskers? He understood that they were rough—but why? And if they are there, why must they go away? On and on it went.

Now I'll be brutally honest and admit that there are some days when this line of questioning really wears me out. When I'm tired or in a hurry, I can easily lose my patience, stifling any hint of curiosity or wonderments my boys might have. I do know that as my years of fathering have grown, so too has my ability to understand and appreciate where the kids are coming from. But I still have my moments.

For most of us, the unrelenting banter of trying to explain even basic things to a youngster is wearying. The patience to explain the *hows* and *whys* of things is something that we mature into. I've also learned that as we grow older, so too do our children, and with this growth comes a greater reluctance to ask questions in the first place.

Have you ever observed a middle school classroom? It is a far cry from the first grade classroom in so many ways, but one of the most evident is the unwillingness of the students to ask about what they do not know. Seventh graders will sit in their seats for days or even months pretending that they fully understand something they don't have a clue about—but the younger learner will almost badger the teacher with questions in an effort to truly get it.

Somewhere in the teen years, our kids (like us before them) become convinced that asking for help or direction is a sign of weakness. In those years of middle and high school, the pressure is so intense to know it all that kids become almost convinced that they do, in fact, know it all. They don't want to appear stupid by asking a question, and they allow their insecurity to blind them to what's really going on around them.

This know-it-all stage is really a new questioning phase. They go from questioning the *hows* and *whys* to just plain questioning everything—their faith, their friends, their circumstances, their parents' choices and decisions. The list goes on and on.

Interestingly, I think it is this form of questioning that many of us take into our relationship with God. We demand to know why things in our life are the way they are. We want answers to why we are married, single, too fat, or too thin. We make choices without considering the consequences and then demand of him an explanation for why we are in a mess. When God doesn't answer us in a timely fashion—or in the way we were expecting—we write it off as God's problem and continue on the path that *we* have chosen to walk.

It took really watching and studying my children to fully understand that God is waiting for me to question him. He allows me to ask questions—questions of the "Daddy, whatcha' doin'?" type.

Have you ever found yourself in the midst of something that you don't understand? A friend of mine moved his family across the country for what he thought was a tremendous job opportunity. The pay was okay and the work was interesting, allowing him to get involved in an organization that was really trying to make a difference in the culture's view of marriage. More importantly, this job offer came at a time when my friend, his wife, and many of our friends had been praying for a new opportunity. It had to be God's will, right?

After thoroughly checking out this new organization, my buddy accepted the job and moved his wife and three children three thousand miles away. Three years later the job was a bust, and they were once again praying for a new direction. What happened?

If you asked my friend, he would tell you that he really doesn't know what the ins and outs of this situation were. He does believe, however, that he failed to ask some critical questions of God the first time around. When the recruiter called, he was so sure that it was his answer to the many prayers that he didn't stop to say, "Hey, God, is this a good thing or a bad thing?" He asked God to work out all of the details, but he didn't stop to ask if the move was the right thing at the time. Bottom line, he didn't seek God's wisdom.

God is aware of our every thought. He is waiting for us to come to him and ask, "What are you doing here? Which path should I take? What's your plan?" before we choose our path. With God, there is no stupid question when we are seeking direction. When we approach him in humility and with an open, seeking heart, he is anxious to offer us guidance. He doesn't respond well to the know-it-all type of questions, and we certainly can't expect to be allowed to demand answers to our questions. But God welcomes our childlike curiosity, understanding that we won't find the answers until we ask the questions.

If any of you lacks wisdom, he should ask God, who gives generously to all without finding fault, and it will be given to him.

JAMES 1:5

45

FATHER'S LOOKING

It was the end-of-the-year celebration in my son's classroom, and parents had been invited to visit. I was late. The fact that I had been held up in traffic didn't matter to my son. All he knew was that the show was starting and I wasn't there. He kept looking, waiting, hoping. I arrived within moments of the opening welcome, and the little guy's face said everything: "Dad, where have you been? I've been waiting and wondering. Thank goodness you're here now!" Obviously, it mattered to him a great deal that I had arrived and would be watching him.

A few weeks later, we were at Johnny's soccer game. He would kick the ball—and then look for me. He would run hard during a play—and then look for me. At one point, he actually got pummeled by another little boy because he was turning to look at me instead of watching the field. It was funny in a not-so-funny kind of way. But even the wallop didn't deter him from seeking me out as he played this game.

I found my son's need for my presence and attention curious. We spend a lot of time together, but in these performance situations Johnny wasn't just looking for my presence. He wanted to know I was watching—that he had my attention and, ultimately, my approval. During the soccer game he knew I was there, but he kept checking to make sure I was actually *seeing* what he was doing. Did I catch that great stop, and was I watching when he popped the ball in for a goal?

As parents, there is that stage during our children's lives when we can do no wrong. Johnny is in that stage right now. He literally thinks the moon rises and sets on his mother and me. Isn't that amazing? He yearns for our approval and attention because we are the center of his little seven-year-old universe. He glows when he hears, "Johnny, you did a great job. I am so pleased." Oh, the immense power of our words on this little boy's heart.

So it is with me and God, my Father. I yearn for his approval in my life. In moments both big and small, I want to know that he is pleased with me—that he is even aware of the choice I've just made or the path I've taken. Of course, God knows all of this. He is completely aware of my need for attention and reminds me that he is watching.

Do you remember in the Book of Luke when Jesus reminds us that we are worth so much to the Father? "Are not five sparrows sold for two pennies? Yet not one of them is forgotten by God. Indeed, the very hairs of your head are all numbered. Don't be afraid; you are worth more than many sparrows" (Luke 12:6–7). This is so amazing to me. God has numbered the hairs on my head! He is so aware of every part of my being, my life, and my every breath that I can't even fathom it.

The tricky part about God's knowledge of me and the choices I make is that he is watching—always! Just as my son wanted to make sure I was giving him my full attention when he was performing, this is my tendency with God. When I'm on a roll, maybe being a particularly great husband or helping an elderly neighbor, I want to call out to him to make sure he's paying attention. "Hey, God, it's me—Johnny. Check this out!"

During those *other* moments that fill my day, well, maybe that can just be a secret between me and my pillow, right? Absolutely not. That's the great part about God. He is watching—always! In Luke, Jesus reminds us that God sees everything. "There is nothing concealed that will not be disclosed, or hidden that will not be made known. What you have said in the dark will be heard in the daylight, and what you have whispered in the ear in the inner rooms will be proclaimed from the roofs" (Luke 12:2–3).

Our natural inclination is to seek God's attention and approval when we're "on"—and to hide in the pillow when we're not. The striking similarity to Johnny amazes me. He was aching for my attention at the soccer game, but in the moments after he spewed some hurtful words to his brother, he was hoping for anything but my attention. I know that he is a work in progress, and he will learn and grow from the guidance I gave him when he wanted to hide in his pillow.

God, our Father, knows that we are works in progress. He is always watching so that in those moments when we make the wrong choice and veer from the path of the righteous, he can draw us near and give us guidance. From God's wisdom, we will learn and grow, and those moments we want to hide in the pillow will become fewer and fewer. He works out each event in our life to bring us closer and closer to becoming the image of his Son. He watches our every step and deed not because he doesn't trust us but because he desires the very best for us.

And we know that in all things God works for the good of those who love him, who have been called according to his purpose. For those God foreknew he also predestined to be conformed to the likeness of his Son.

ROMANS 8:28–29

46

WISHING THE TIME AWAY

There are many things about being a child that I really don't remember very well, but one thing that's very clear is the memory of always wishing and waiting for the next stage. Whatever was going on in my life paled in comparison to what I knew must await me around the next corner. Wishing the time away started so very early in my life that I think it must be somehow ingrained in the human flesh to always be looking down the road at what is coming instead of enjoying the scenery right where one is.

In the "olden days," as my sons have come to call them, we didn't have kindergarten, so first grade was my first look-ahead moment. I have no idea what was going on in my life when I was five, but boy, I couldn't wait to be six so that I could go to the big school! Once I got there, of course, I couldn't wait for summer. This became a comfortable pattern for me and thousands of other children—anticipating the start of a new school year only to turn all of my attention to the vacation that was somewhere down the road.

Ten was a big year. Somehow I knew that turning ten would mean all kinds of magical, wonderful things for me. But once I turned ten, I couldn't wait to be twelve, and then I was looking forward so much to thirteen. Once I hit the teens, none mattered except sixteen. Of course that came with the privilege to drive, but once I got my license, eighteen became my focus. Ahh, eighteen, now that was a year I knew without question would hold something I couldn't even begin to imagine—independence, the right to vote, leaving home, and going away to college. At eighteen the whole world would open up, and I, Johnny, would become a completely different person. I was just sure that life really couldn't get any better than it would be when I was eighteen—until I turned eighteen and started looking toward the magical age of twenty-one.

It is almost tragic to think of all the joy and potential for growth I missed along the way because I was so doggedly looking down the road at what might be. Of course, the constant reminder from grown-ups in my life, "Johnny, don't wish your life away," held no meaning until I became the grown-up. Now that *my* child is eagerly waiting for the next great moment in life, I see it all so differently.

My oldest son had just celebrated his eighth birthday. It was a great day that included family, friends, presents, and an unbelievably good cake! I remember going to bed that night thinking that my son would remember this great day for a long time. Imagine my shock and surprise when he woke up the next morning talking about next year! His focus wasn't on enjoying the new toys he'd received or basking in the glow of what a great celebration we'd had. His eyes were on how his ninth birthday party would be different from this one. "Not that this one was bad, Dad," he wanted to be sure I understood, "but next year. . . ."

As my boy finished listing the grand plans he had in mind for his upcoming birthday, only twelve months away, I heard myself saying, "Don't wish your life away, son." But I could tell from the glazed look on his face that my words meant nothing to him. He couldn't begin to grasp what I was saying, and truthfully, I don't blame him. This is one of those things you really can't even begin to understand until many more years have passed. So I left him with his dreams and started thinking about the holes we are continually trying to fill. I think we struggle in our lives to enjoy the journey because we are convinced the destination holds something life-changing. We may be unhappy in this moment, but if we can only get to "Destination X," everything will be different.

As a child, the magical destination is often an upcoming birthday or school vacation, but for those of us in the grown-up world, "Destination X" can be many different things.

Do you remember thinking, "This really isn't how my life is supposed to be going, but once I get married . . . "? This line of thinking is so commonplace in today's world. As singles, we are convinced that we will finally be somebody once we have somebody—only to find out that getting married doesn't really change who we are.

A friend was telling me one day that he just couldn't wait for his next big promotion because that was where all the glory was. "Once I get that job, Johnny, I'm on the road. I will finally have the life I've always wanted."

Whatever we see down the road, we are convinced it will somehow alter the *very essence* of who we are and how life is treating us. Whether it's a new job, a raise, a cross-country move, or even a new special person in our lives, we wrap all our hopes and dreams up in that future moment or event, passing on what might be in store for us in the very day we are living. As children, it's hard to see how any of this matters, but as adults, it's important for us to remember that God wants us to live in the present, focusing on the journey he has for us.

When we are focused on the future, we are saying, "God, what you're giving me isn't enough. It's not what I need. I'll just take care of it myself." The classic example of this is Eve in the Garden. She has absolutely everything one could possibly imagine wanting, but when the serpent tempts her with the knowledge from the Tree of Life, she can't resist opening herself up to something better and bolder than what God had planned for her. Remember Abraham and Sarah? They desperately wanted a child. God told Abraham more than once that he would provide an heir in *his* time, but Abraham tired of waiting. He took matters into his own hands, fathering a child with Hagar, which led to great unrest throughout history.

In Matthew 6, Jesus tells us not to worry *about anything:* "Do not worry about your life, what you will eat or drink; or about your body, what you will wear. . . . Look at the birds of the air; they do not sow or reap or store away in barns, and yet your heavenly Father feeds them. Are you not much more valuable than they? Who of you by worrying can add a single hour to his life? . . . Do not worry about tomorrow, for tomorrow will worry about itself. Each day has enough trouble of its own" (vv. 25–27, 34).

Clearly, Jesus is telling us that each day has plenty in it to keep us fully focused, and that our job is to seek God's kingdom and his righteousness each day, letting God take care of tomorrow.

Living in the moment requires that we let go of *our* wants, *our* time, *our* priorities. It demands that we submit our lives to God's plan, remembering that we will be given exactly what we are ready for. He will not ask us to go through something we are not prepared to handle, and likewise, he will not give us something for which we are not yet ready to be responsible. If you think you're ready for that big raise, go to God and talk to him about it. He will provide for you in *his* time. Do not take matters into your own hands. Time and time again, thinking we know what is best for tomorrow will catch us in a snare.

God has a plan. Leave tomorrow to him, knowing that he is a God of trust and promise. Live this day to its fullest with faith that in the hand of God, tomorrow is already taken care of. Let's not spend our days wishing them all away!

This is the day the LORD has made; let us rejoice and be glad in it.

PSALM 118:24

47

GOD'S NEEDLES—Rx FOR GOOD SPIRITUAL HEALTH

Some things never change. We did not enjoy hypodermic needles as kids, and we do not like them now. Neither do our children. Yet hypodermic needles play a vital role in our health. Some needles are designed to draw blood so it can be examined for impurities. Other needles are necessary for immunization, to protect us from diseases.

Needle day at the doctor's office is never easy for Johnny, Jordan, and Joel (or for Mom and Dad, for that matter). As parents we've learned to tag team this event, applying half nelsons, at times, as needed. Predictably, before the doctor walks in, the tears fall down. Our sons display a Pavlovian response to what they know is coming.

We have developed the practice of not shaming them by making comments such as, "Now be a big boy. . . . Don't cry . . . Just suck it up." Instead we lovingly hold them as they squirm and scream. Often we begin weeping with them because we know the initial entry point (no pun intended) can be the toughest.

I have often wondered what they're thinking at those moments. Perhaps they question inwardly,

"Why are my parents letting the doctor hurt me?"
"Why can't I run away?"
"Do I have to?"

The boys have yet to count it all joy. After the ordeal, they have yet to say to us, "Thanks to both of you for allowing me to experience this. I will be a better and healthier child because of this. I am forever grateful."

At their ages, they do not understand the necessity and purpose of the periodic doctor visits, but perhaps, as the old hymn says, they'll "understand it better by and by."

When the doctor is finished, my sons usually receive a reward—a lollipop. Not great for nutritional value, but it does wonders for the attitude!

The Great Physician also uses needles—they are called trials and tribulations. The Spirit of God x-rays our lives and scans our hearts, searching for emotional fractures (unmended hearts) and spiritual contamination (idols in our lives). All things are naked to the Spirit, for he is able to divide the joints and marrow and discern the thoughts and intents of the heart (Heb. 4:12–13). Trials are designed to expose our pride, hypocrisies, and self-reliance. God allows them to penetrate our lives—not to destroy, but to develop and mold us into the image of Christ. God, in his love, permits his children to be bruised—he allows our lives to be pricked with thorny experiences in order to build strong character. He applies divine radiation to spiritually infected areas.

In the Great Physician's hands, the prognosis is always good. Still, we must continually perform routine self-examinations for the sake of early problem detection. We must ask bold health questions, such as,

"Am I growing more or less in love with Jesus?"
"What am I pretending not to see in my life and relationships?"
"How did I treat people today?"

"Is there anyone I need to forgive?"

"Are there any spiritual diseases such as arrogance, greed, or unresolved anger surrounding my heart?"

The Great Physician measures the serum in the tube, not permitting it to be filled with more than we can bear. He allows the appropriate amount to be dispensed in order to do the work of forming Christ in us. But in order for the needles to be truly effective, every drop must be fully injected into our lives. Perseverance must then do its work in the veins of our circumstances so that we may be mature and complete (receiving a good bit of health).

At the end, the Great Physician rewards us with something far sweeter and longer lasting than a lollipop. He gives a crown that reads:

Blessed is the man who perseveres under trial, because when he has stood the test, he will receive the crown of life that God has promised to those who love him.

JAMES 1:12

48

HOW COME GOD LETS THE WIND BLOW SO HARD?

One night I was lying in bed with one of my sons during our bedtime routine, and the wind was howling so loudly outside his window, I could almost feel it reaching inside my soul. Oh, how those winter winds can howl! As he snuggled ever closer to me, he asked me why God let the wind blow so hard. "Is there a tornado outside? Will the wind blow our house down?" he wanted to know.

I did my best that night to reassure him, reminding him that our house was built on a strong foundation that could withstand the strength of the storm outside. I told him we would be okay because God was looking after us. I reminded him that God is always with us—even when the wind blows. My words were fine, but he really just needed me—my physical presence made him feel secure. I stayed with him a good part of the night to help him rest and to bring some calm to his troubled heart.

As we lay there in his little bed, I found myself thinking about Jesus being called *Immanuel, God with us.* God allows the storm and the winds to come into our lives, but he promises to be with us in the storm and in the winds—he is *Immanuel, God with us*. God's presence doesn't stop the winds from howling outside our door. They roar in the form of adversity and trials—hard times that, if we're honest, we'd rather not have in our lives.

Years ago, the wind was blowing hard in my own life. I was just completing my first book, and I was consumed by every little detail of the process. It almost felt like I was giving birth—figuratively of course—and I was gripped by the throes of postpartum depression. I've never felt that bleak and dark in my life. I didn't even know it was possible to drop so low. There were moments when I would cry out to God, asking him to allow me the blessing of tears just so I could get my emotions out. My wife loved me patiently through that dark season, praying all the while for my relief.

It came one day through a phone call. I was just heading out the door when the phone rang, so I let the answering machine pick up. I stopped cold when I heard the caller's voice ring through my house. It was my friend Tom, who lived out west and who had served as a mentor in my life. I hadn't talked to Tom in over a year, and when I ran to pick up the phone, Tom's voice was like a glass of cold water in the heat of the desert. I began to pour out to Tom what I was thinking and feeling, what I was going through. He tenderly listened, allowing me to release every emotion that had been locked inside of me somehow.

Why this call at this moment? How did Tom know? What led him to call me? *Immanuel, God with us.* Tom's call was Jesus being with me. It was *Immanuel, God with us,* reaching out to me through the voice of a trusted friend. *Immanuel, God with us,* showing himself faithful. God used Tom to minister to me and to restore me to emotional health. He brought Tom to me that day to help rev up the emotional needle on the dashboard of my heart from empty to full again. The wind was still blowing, but I had bold hope and a new perspective.

When Peter got out of the boat and walked on water, he was fine as long as his eyes were on Jesus, Immanuel. As soon as he took his eyes off Jesus and began looking at the wind blowing, he began to sink. You may be asking at this very moment, "Why does God allow the wind to blow?" The question I ask is, "Where are your eyes? Are you looking at the wind, or are you looking at Immanuel? Are you looking at the fact that he is with you, or are you wondering where he is?" Look closely. God is there. Maybe he's with you through a friend's phone call or e-mail or through a book you're reading, or through a song, Scripture verse, or sermon. Just look around. How are you experiencing *Immanuel, God with you,* today?

Have I not commanded you? Be strong and courageous. Do not be terrified; do not be discouraged, for the Lord your God will be with you wherever you go.

JOSHUA 1:9

139

49

KEEP KNOCKING

Daddy, Daddy, Daddy!" Does this sound familiar? The loud and demanding voice of a three-year-old who wants my attention, not in five minutes, not in one minute, but now, thank you. There are times when I enjoy this, but when I arrive home from work, I need twenty minutes or so to unwind and "sift," as my wife calls it.

As my routine goes, I like to read the mail. Usually, it's just bills and advertisements from companies I've never heard of. But you never know, maybe someday the mail will hold unexpected money or a warm greeting from an old friend.

Having finished the mail, I feel compelled to check for any phone messages or exciting e-mails. Again there are the usual culprits, but maybe one day there will be an invitation from someone asking me to speak at a marriage retreat in the Cayman Islands.

Clearly, during these first twenty minutes or so in the door, I am in "unwind" mode, and my mind is working its way toward the home front. But my son has his own agenda. He insists on having my attention, and he won't quit pulling at my pants leg until he has my full, undivided focus. Realizing I'm engaged in a losing battle, I acknowledge him by saying, "Yes, Joel," but this doesn't satisfy him. He continues to yank and pull for several minutes until I bend down to get at his eye level where he grabs my head and makes me look him right in the face, eye to eye. Satisfied that he now has my full attention, he says, "Daddy, can I have some candy?" There are just some parenting moments that I really don't think I'll ever understand!

Did you know that God is never distracted? We never have to worry that he's more focused on the mail than on us. We don't have to think for even a brief moment of pulling on his pant leg, because he is always ready and waiting for us to come to him for conversation.

God can hear prayers from Sydney, Australia, and Beltsville, Maryland, at the same time. He can care for the person suffering with cancer and the man who just lost his job without missing a beat. God is never overwhelmed with our big requests, yet there is no concern too small for him to listen to either. God wants us to nag him, to be constantly knocking at heaven's door. It is a living picture of our faith in his awesome power.

The story of the man who goes to a neighbor's house begging for bread at midnight is a good example. The owner gives bread just to shut the man up. This man knew where the bread could be found, and he wouldn't quit until he got an answer. His persistence was out of need. Many times ours is out of greed or something unhealthy. He wanted to see the owner face-to-face and let his need be known. To keep asking with the right petitions—and right heart motivation—gets God's attention. So keep knocking at the right door and let your needs be known. God won't give whatever we want just to quiet us. He will lovingly examine our situation. Sometimes he will say "No," sometimes "Grow," sometimes "Slow," and other times "Go."

Ask and it will be given to you; seek and you will find; knock and the door will be opened to you.

MATTHEW 7:7

50

WHAT ABOUT HIM?

Okay, let's just say it all together now: "Life's not fair!" I've heard it about twenty times just in this day alone.

My oldest got the last of the favored cereal at breakfast, right before my youngest used the last drop of fresh strawberry jam. Neither of those lasts was fair in the minds of the two who missed out.

My oldest son had tennis lessons—of course, that's not fair, because why can't the other two have them at the same time?

By lunchtime, it was the milk that someone drained just before another was going to pour a second glass—that's not fair either.

And now, one child *gets* to empty the dishwasher while the other two *have* to fold laundry. You guessed it, that's not fair.

I'm sure by the time bedtime rolls around later tonight, there will be a whole list of other injustices in the minds of the children.

Shall we say it all together again? "Life's not fair!"

Of course, the question begging to be asked is, "Fair by whose standard?" There really is little fair about the world. Deceit is rewarded with higher office. Betrayal is met with a wink and a nod. Compromise is rewarded with a bigger car and a mansion on the lake.

Or so our human minds tell us. Are our minds where our standard is set and, therefore, judged? Are we to look around us and determine our course in life by what we see others doing? I think the Scriptures are clear about this. Remember when Jesus was reinstating Peter? Peter is so focused on John that in response to Jesus' direction to him, Peter asks, "Lord, what about him?" and Jesus said, "What is that to you?" (John 21:21–22). It was not Peter's business to know what was going to happen to John or how their roles were different. Peter's business was Peter—and how he was responding to Jesus' direction.

God makes it very clear that, just like Peter, our focus is to be on ourselves and not on those around us. In 2 Corinthians, the message is very clear: "We do not dare to classify or compare ourselves with some who commend themselves. When they measure themselves by themselves and compare themselves with themselves, they are not wise" (10:12). We have differing bodies, gifts, and blessings by God's design, and he is not pleased when we play the comparison game. God loves us all the same, but we are not all treated the same.

I have had moments in my life when I have had to drag myself out of a pity party. I put myself in God's place, thinking I know it all. I dwell on the man next to me on the freeway in the expensive car or the man on the street who lives a sin-filled life but has great material reward. I have found myself thinking, "Why him, Lord? I try so hard, work so hard. . . . What about me?" How quickly I must repent of my own sin, taking the timber out of my own eye lest I truly receive justice for the thoughts and actions of my own sin-filled life.

Our God is a just God, and he knows the heart of every man, woman, and child. I need to remember that it is only through his grace that I don't receive what I truly deserve. Better that I focus on my own heart and mind than the car next to me on the freeway. Life isn't always the way we want it to be, and it doesn't always seem fair from our perspective. But with God, all is fair and all is just. We have to fight our urge to doubt or question because he is the Lord of lords, and he is in control.

"Lord, what about him?" Jesus answered . . . "What is that to you?"

JOHN 21:21–22

143

51

IN A PERFECT WORLD?

I just laughed as a friend of mine told me, "Walking across the playroom in my basement is like crossing a minefield right now. My kids have the Playmobil town everywhere! Ack!"

Now for those of you not familiar with Playmobil, they are tiny plastic pieces in the forms of people, animals, cars, buildings, and most anything else you can think of. The kids spend hours setting it up and then delve into some sort of make-believe adventure.

My friend's nine-year-old daughter has quite a collection of these tiny pieces. She told her dad, "I love Playmobil because everything is perfect. Everyone gets things exactly the way they want them when they want them." A perfect world—now there's a thought.

My children have an amazingly blessed life, and yet it seems almost second nature for them to dwell on how things could be better. For my son, *perfect* means no bedtime, cheese pizza for every meal, and unlimited amounts of vanilla milk shakes. The list expands when a new toy comes out that he just *has* to have, and it changes a bit with each birthday, but all in all, these things represent his perfect world.

Do you have an idea of perfect? For many adults, a perfect world might involve their career goals, the size of their home, or the size of their bank account. For us, perfect can tend to be about *things* and, just like the kids with the Playmobil, we can spend hours, months, or even years dreaming of what it will be like when we can have everything we want when we want it.

God is only too aware of our propensity to dwell on what we do not have. How do I know this? Because in Philippians we are told that being content is something that we *learn*. Why do we have to learn contentment? Because God knows that our human nature, if left to its own course, will choose a path of focusing on what we do not have instead of focusing on all with which we are blessed.

Philippians 4:11–13 says, "I have learned to be content whatever the circumstances. I know what it is to be in need, and I know what it is to have plenty. I have learned the secret of being content in any and every situation, whether well fed or hungry, whether living in plenty or in want. I can do everything through him who gives me strength." What Paul is teaching us in this passage is that contentment has absolutely nothing to do with what we have. It isn't about material things, food, clothing, or even our health. Rather, it is a statement of our trust in God's provision. No matter the circumstance, when we trust God to provide for our needs, our focus will be on all he does for us, not on what we do not have.

Just think about Paul as he wrote those words in Philippians. He was in prison, having suffered terribly for his ministry. But Paul did not focus on his jail cell or his plight. He kept his focus on God, choosing to look up instead of around. He gives us the key to contentment *no matter* our circumstances: "I can do everything through him who gives me strength" (Phil. 4:13). No matter what life brings you, if you look up instead of around, believing that God can and will give you the strength to endure, you will find contentment.

I have learned to be content whatever the circumstances. I know what it is to be in need, and I know what it is to have plenty. I have learned the secret of being content in any and every situation, whether well fed or hungry, whether living in plenty or in want. I can do everything through him who gives me strength.

PHILIPPIANS 4:11–13

52

JUST LIKE RIDING A BIKE

On my sixth birthday, my parents bought me the most wonderful bike—a royal blue Schwinn that sparkled in the sunlight. It had this amazing white banana-shaped seat that also sparkled. I remember the sparkles were actually embedded in the plastic material. It was one of the most treasured gifts I ever received.

Riding that beautiful bike seemed like it would be so simple. I convinced my parents that I didn't need training wheels, and they watched with that bemused look I now understand much better than I did then! Out the door I went, hopped on, and promptly crashed. Luckily, I was on the lawn, and the physical damage was minimal.

It took weeks with my dad running behind me before I was finally able to pedal on my own. He would say, "I'm going to let go," and I would yell, "No, Daddy, I can't do it without you!" He would let go—and I would fall, over and over again. Finally, that magical moment came. He let go—and I kept going.

Now it is my turn to run behind the bike. My son, too, has no fear and is sure he can master this task on his own. Just like those who have gone before him, he has crashed over and over

146

again. Each day we head out the door thinking, *This will be the day.*

It is an odd mix of emotion to want to be free so badly and yet to fear being set free. My son says, "No, Daddy, don't let go. I'm going to fall." I resist letting go because I don't want him to fall, yet I know the only way for him to ride is for me to let go, and so I release him. One day very soon, he will keep going, all on his own. That wonderful look that says, "I did it!" will fill his face, and I will feel my heart skip a beat, knowing that together we have achieved success.

Throughout my life, I know without a doubt that God has held on to the back of my "bike"—a lot! In the early days of my faith, God was holding me up almost exclusively. I knew that I wanted to devote my life to him, but I didn't know how. As I wobbled precariously, his steady hand guided me. He drew me to his Word, showing me that it was a treasure filled with guiding principles for my life. He led me to a church community and provided a godly mentor who helped me navigate the sometimes stormy waters of life.

As my strength grew, God was able to release me for moments when I would balance on my own. As his hand prepared to withdraw, I would think, "No, please, don't let go. I'm going to fall." But God, in his infinite wisdom, knew that I would be okay. Yes, I might crash and burn, but he would be right there to pick me up and give me the courage to get back on the "bike."

God says, "I know the plans I have for you" (Jer. 29:11), and he will guide us in a perfect way if we allow him to. He will hold on to us when that is what we need; he will gently let go of us when it is our time to coast a bit; and sometimes he will completely let go and watch us ride freely. He will not allow us to crash and burn needlessly. Just as a few bumps and bruises were part of my son learning to master his bicycle, so it is with us. We will go through some hard patches on our way to Christlike perfection. It is all part of the Father's plan to draw us nearer to him.

Can you picture God's radiant face as he watches you? It is for him as it was for me as my son strove to master his bike. I knew what joy was ahead of him once he truly became a bike rider. In those moments of despair, when he wanted to leave the bike on the hard sidewalk where he had just crashed, I encouraged him because I knew what was ahead. We overcame his fear, his frustration, and his moments of temporary failure, and together we were successful. So it is with God. He knows what is ahead of us, and if we will rely on him to carry us through our fear, frustration, and moments of failure, together we will achieve great things.

"For I know the plans I have for you," declares the LORD, *"plans to prosper you and not to harm you, plans to give you hope and a future."*

JEREMIAH 29:11

53

GETTING LIFE TO FIT

N o, Daddy, I can do it myself!"—the words that every parent hears from his or her child for the first time somewhere between the ages of one and three. I remember the moment my firstborn uttered this phrase. At the time, I thought it was wonderful. "Hmm, he can do it himself? Wow, we must be entering some newer, easier version of parenting if he can really do things for himself."

The joke was clearly on me. As any seasoned parent could have told me, this was just the beginning of a battle of wills that would go on for years to come.

One of the first glimpses I had into the potential pitfalls of "I can do it myself" was when my son was not quite three. It was a bitterly cold Virginia morning, and my son needed his coat to head out the door. I grabbed his coat from the hook and offered a sleeve for his waiting arm—except his arm wasn't waiting. It was glued to his side. Thinking we were going to have some sort of a game, I chuckled and said, "Come on, son; put your arm in the hole." He looked me straight in the eye and said, "No, Daddy, I can do it myself."

Okay, I thought, *I have time for this today. I'll just teach him how to put his coat on by himself.* I hear you giggling because, of course, you know that the last thing my son wanted was for me to *teach* him anything on that cold morning. He resisted my efforts to work with him, continually saying, "I do it myself . . . I do it myself. . . ." For the next ten minutes or so he struggled to put his jacket on while I quietly watched from my perch on the stairs. Finally, he became frustrated and slammed his jacket down on the floor. His sweet little brown eyes turned up to me, and holding in a quickly approaching sob, he quietly said, "Daddy, I can't. Will you help me?" What an amazing picture he was of the lifelong struggle we have to accept God's teaching and will for our lives.

Over and over again, the Scripture reminds us of God's concern for us. Isaiah 58:11 says, "The LORD will guide you always; he will satisfy your needs in a sun-scorched land and will strengthen your frame. You will be like a well-watered garden, like a spring whose waters never fail." John 6:35 reminds us that in Jesus, our every need is taken care of: "I am the bread of life. He who comes to me will never go hungry, and he who believes in me will never be thirsty." Listen to the sweet words of Philippians 4:19: "And my God will meet all your needs according to his glorious riches in Christ Jesus." God wants to help us. He offers time and time again, but in our pride, we resist him, just as my son resisted me.

Sometimes God will allow us to have what we think we want. Think of Israel's fate in the Old Testament. After the time of the judges, God provided Israel a prophet, priest, and judge in Samuel, who was a man of God. Samuel would do what was right in God's eyes, but the Israelites weren't satisfied. They wanted a king like other nations had, and with this plea, the Israelites denied the Lord as their king. God knew full well what the path of a monarchy would bring to the nation of Israel, but he allowed the Israelites to have what they thought they wanted. It brought them great woe.

God says to us, "Let me teach you how to live, how to parent, how to be married, how to be a friend," but we reply, "No, Daddy, I can do it myself!" As with the children of Israel, God will allow pain and frustration to occur so that we surrender to him. It could all be so simple. When my son surrendered to me for help with his jacket, it took me just a few seconds to show him how to get it on. How many more struggles will we have that are rooted in will and pride? And so it is with my heavenly Father and me. It would be so much simpler if I would just do it his way to begin with—but, oh, for my human flesh.

It grieves God to watch us struggle, to see us in agony, but he knows the greater good that awaits us once we turn to him. He loves to hear us say, "Daddy, I can't do it. Will you help me, please?"

Oh, that my ways were steadfast in obeying your decrees!

PSALM 119:5

54

CAN'T WE JUST ALL GET ALONG?

It was one of those memorable parenting moments—all three boys playing together and liking it! I'm not sure if it's the dynamics of having three children or just the reality of siblings, but these moments don't come along as often as I would like. It seems that more often than not, one child is on the outside of the loop. While this gives me many teachable moments, it also gets wearisome at times. Why can't they just all get along?

Boy, don't you think that is exactly what God wonders? He creates this beautiful world for us to live in. He gives us blessing on top of blessing. Yet we find more things to disagree over than one can possibly imagine. It is almost as if we look upon his blessings as burdens, not taking the time to fully appreciate the great gifts we have all around us.

As a parent, watching my boys get along and be kind to one another, whether watching television or playing a game, brings me joy. When the kids are on the same page, there's oneness, unity, and harmony. It brings me deep satisfaction to see this.

How much more is the Father's heart overflowing with joy when he sees his earthly children treating each other with tenderness and love, living in one accord and harmony? Psalm 133 tells us how dearly the Father holds our unity:

> How good and pleasant it is
> when brothers live together in unity!
> It is like precious oil poured on the head,
> running down on the beard,
> running down on Aaron's beard,
> down upon the collar of his robes.
> It is as if the dew of Hermon
> were falling on Mount Zion,
> For there the LORD bestows his blessing,
> even life forevermore.

How wonderful, how beautiful, when brothers and sisters get along!

PSALM 133:1 MESSAGE

THE TEN(DER) COMMANDMENTS

When we read the Ten Commandments, many people think of God as a harsh, angry old man in the sky who's saying, "If you get out of line with these commandments, I'm going to grill you like a burger on a hot summer day." We think the commandments are harsh, unloving, confining, and restrictive. But really they're not. They are the *tender* commandments. They are really God's love given through boundaries he set down for us to live within.

I love my children. I tell them, "I don't want you to play outside in the street. I don't want you to talk with strangers. I don't want you wandering away from me in the mall." I give them these instructions not because I want to confine them or rob them of joy but because I want to protect them.

When we read all those "Thou shalt not's," I think we get overwhelmed. When God says things like "don't steal ... don't kill ... don't covet and lust for something that's not yours ... don't get involved with someone else's spouse and commit adultery," it's not because God's a killjoy who wants to confine us. He wants us to be free, and he knows that if we live within his boundaries, we can live freely. The things he is trying to protect us from will destroy and kill us. God has created spiritual laws within the universe, and if we break these laws, they're going to bring pain.

You know if you're on the tenth floor of a building and you jump out the window, you are going to drop down because of the physical law of gravity. It doesn't matter if you're black or white, rich or poor, Christian or non-Christian, your fall will be governed by the law. The same is true in the spiritual realm. You're going to experience pain if you defy the spiritual laws God has put in place.

One day I saw my infant son, Joel, crawl across the floor and pull himself up on a big pot with a plant in it. He immediately stuck his hands in the dirt and the dirt into his mouth. Now I could have just sat and watched this all happen—it was quite a sight after all—but Joel wasn't designed to eat dirt. It just wasn't a good option for him, and as his father, it's my job to intervene. At eight months of age, his natural instinct is to check out the dirt. As the Dad, I had to say, "Joel, no, you can't eat dirt; this is not good." Now that Joel is three, I have to intervene in the exact same way between Joel and the candy bowl. "Joel, no, you can't eat that much candy because you'll get holes in your teeth and a monstrous tummy ache!"

This is how God puts boundaries of love around us. We're diving headfirst into a relationship and have lost our way. God steps in and says, "No, I don't want you to be involved sexually. There is nothing but pain involved without a loving, committed covenant relationship. Let me protect you." Or maybe we're in over our head at work and a gentle lie combined with a bit of gossip is just what will fix the situation. God again steps in, saying, "No. I don't want you to be someone who doesn't tell the truth. There's pain in being a liar and a gossip. Let me protect you."

We are all strong, self-driven people, and it is hard to allow ourselves to be held accountable to any set of rules—even when they're from God. But the next time you find yourself resisting, remember that God puts loving boundaries around us not to confine us but to set us free. The Ten Commandments are really one of the most tender things our all-knowing and all-loving God could have done for us—allowing us to live a life free for his glory.

The law of the LORD is perfect, reviving the soul. The statutes of the LORD are trustworthy, making wise the simple.

PSALM 19:7

56

BEHAVIORS THAT NAG

We all had our childhood issues. I have a friend who was a thumb sucker. She has no idea why or how, but she remembers her mother's secret fear that she would "go to school sucking that thumb," as she used to say. Her mother tried everything—Tabasco, hot pepper, Vaseline. Nothing worked, because as a young girl, my friend would immediately go to the bathroom, wash her thumb, and promptly stick it back in her mouth. Then one day the summer before heading off to school, she just stopped. She says, "I have no idea how or why. I just didn't want or need to suck my thumb anymore, much to my poor mother's relief!"

My son is not a thumb sucker. His issue has been wetting the bed. To be honest, I think this whole thing bothered me more than it did him in the beginning. He would wake up uncomfortable, enlist my help to fix the immediate problem, and then fall promptly back to sleep. I, on the other hand, would be rousted from my sleep and have to wake up enough to do the cleaning, changing, and retucking. Just enough of my adrenaline would start pumping that it would take me awhile to fall back asleep, resulting in a hard wake-up come morning. I tried everything—talking him through it, cutting off all liquids early in the evening, even waking him up for one last chance to empty his bladder just before I went to bed. Nothing seemed to help, and for quite a while, he really didn't seem to give it much thought.

Then the other night he came up to me and said, "Dad, I just prayed and asked God to help me not wet the bed anymore." I was so touched because he had reached a point in his life where this was really becoming an issue he wanted to deal with and he knew to turn to God. Sure enough, though, early the next morning, before the sun rose, my son woke me, and I could tell immediately that he had had an accident. My reaction surprised me. As I crawled out of bed, I was filled with compassion instead of irritability. My heart ached for this little guy because I knew he was filled with shame and embarrassment. Even worse, because he had shared with me his prayer to God about this very issue, I sensed his feelings of failure.

After cleaning the little guy up and tucking him for a bit more sleep, I found myself thinking about Psalm 103. It says, "As a father has compassion on his children, so the LORD has compassion on those who fear him; for he knows how we are formed, he remembers that we are dust" (vv. 13–14).

The whole experience I had just had with my son was a picture of God! How many of us, as adults, have struggles? Do you have nagging habits in your life that no one else really knows about because you are embarrassed and ashamed of them? Maybe you smoke cigarettes but know that you shouldn't—so you only smoke on the back porch in the dark of night so no one can see you. Maybe you have an emotional connectedness to a coworker that your gut is telling you isn't quite right—but it seems okay as long as your spouse doesn't sense it. Maybe it's gossip—that urge to chat about the teacher when all of the parents get together. We all have our issues.

The good news is that, just like my son, most of us have a sincere desire to conquer our habit and move on. And God is there for us! He sees our hearts, and he has compassion on us as we come before him. This is the key—that we come before God with humble, sincere hearts, and ask him to help us conquer our nagging habits.

When my son had his accident that night after praying, he didn't try to hide it. Rather, he came to me in sincerity and sadness that it happened again. This is what God wants from us. When we approach him about our nagging habit with sincerity of heart, he has compassion on us.

What are those behaviors in you that keep happening over and over again? As you begin to think about them, be encouraged that God, your heavenly Father, cares about each and every issue you have. Run to him. Pour out your heart to him. He is waiting with open, compassionate arms to help you. He will clothe you anew, helping you set a new course for a life lived worthy of his honor.

If we confess our sins, he is faithful and just and will forgive us our sins and purify us from all unrighteousness.

1 JOHN 1:9

57

REMEMBER WHO
YOU ARE

In the 1970s, New York City was notorious for its gangs. One popular gang was the Seven Crowns. You knew who they were by the colors they wore, the way they swaggered when they walked, and the song they sang about their gang. Clearly they filled a gaping void in the lives of their young adherents. In a twisted, dysfunctional way, they were connected and felt a profound sense of unity. They felt a belonging and cultivated an identity based on an ungodly, unrighteous lifestyle. They were family, exerting more influence over their devotees than their families of origin.

Studies show that scores of kids flock to gangs in order to experience the family they never had. Gangs are often in the right place at the right time and offer themselves as a nurturing, caring community in which members are affirmed and protected from the cold, cruel world. The most well-known gang, the Mafia, often refers to itself as *Cosa Nostra*, "our family." To our shame, gangs provide a sense of belonging and identity for which the kids in our families are starving.

In my family, we have tried to take what gangs have meant for evil and convert it into good. Periodically I assume the role of a marine drill sergeant and line up my boys as if they were a platoon. After they are lined up in front of me, I begin going through the routine:

"Who are we, boys?"

They reply, "We are Parker men."

"Whom do we love?"

"We love Jesus!"

"Whom else do we love?"

"We love our family, our mommy and daddy."

Then I ask, "How do we treat people?"

"We treat people with honor."

Next, as we swipe our noses (because there is always something dripping from little boys' noses), we say simultaneously, "Yeah, we are Parker men."

Although I am lovingly in their faces, I want this concept to get into their hearts. I understand that the boot camp of character development and identity formation is the family. This is critical. As parents, we are the ones to form our children's identity. In our family, for example, we do not call our sons "bad boys" when they misbehave. Instead, we say they have made "bad choices." We want them to understand that their identity is in Jesus Christ. That can never change, no matter how tall they may grow, no matter how athletic they may become, no matter how good their grades might be. What will never change will be the fact that in Jesus they are loved, they are valued, they are accepted, and they are secure. "Though my father and mother forsake me, the LORD will receive me" (Ps. 27:10).

Our identity in Christ is a sure thing—as sure as money in the bank. In Matthew 3:17, when Jesus came up out of the water from his baptism, the Father said, "This is my Son, whom I love; with him I am well pleased." These are the same words the Father speaks to you and me today, words that shape our identity. Anew, today, he says, "I am well pleased." We have the security that in him we are loved, that he is well pleased with us—not based on performance, but based on the fact that we are his children in Jesus Christ. We are joint heirs with Christ.

God says to us, "You are joint heirs with Jesus. You are the salt of the earth. You are saints. This is your identity. Remember who you are. You belong to me. You are my beloved son in whom I am well pleased."

This is affirmation at its finest, the answer to the silent scream of every child's heart, to know their identity and to know they are pleasing in the eyes of their earthly parents. More than that, they need ultimate affirmation in the eyes of their heavenly Father. Next time someone asks you how you are doing, you should tell them you are "well pleased" because of who you are in your Father's eyes and because of whose you are.

If we live, we live to the Lord; and if we die, we die to the Lord. So, whether we live or die, we belong to the Lord.

ROMANS 14:8

58

WHEN I GET BIGGER

The son of a friend of mine had been waiting to grow for months, and this summer, finally, has been his time. He had been consumed by his size. He would say, "I have these big feet. I'm sure I will be big when I grow up." But the mark on the wall, which he checked weekly for an entire year, stubbornly refused to move . . . and then it did. He shot up almost four inches in three months, just in time to keep his younger sibling from passing him by. "Whew!"

Children—especially little boys—are focused on their size. If you listen closely to a group of little boys playing, you'll hear them say things like, "When I get bigger, I'm gonna be . . ." or "Just wait until I get bigger!" My son considers it a great accomplishment to be able to touch the doorjamb as he passes through it or that his head almost reaches his mother's chin. It seems almost inbred, a child's desire to grow taller and bigger—in a physical sense. And amazingly, grow they will, with little help from us. Sure, we feed and water them, trying to help them make healthy choices when it comes to food, sleep, and exercise, but physical growth is just part of the deal.

Much more complicated is helping our children *grow*. By this I mean finding their purpose in life and the path for achieving it. I really believe that it's the job of significant people in children's lives to fan the flame of their purpose. I once heard someone say that there are two great events in our lives: the day we are born and the day we discover *why* we were born—why we're supposed to get bigger. Wouldn't it be something to hear those little boys say, "When I get bigger, I'm going to be a man of integrity." Wow, what a parenting moment!

It is said of Jesus that he grew in favor with God and man. This principle of purpose applies not only to our children but to us. God is not just interested in our becoming bigger in terms of physical size; he wants us to grow bigger in terms of our faith, bigger in terms of our love and our commitment and intimacy with him. How have you been growing lately? Have you been placing yourself in situations where you can develop and grow in your faith and your intimacy with God? Here's to setting a purpose for getting bigger!

And we pray this in order that you may live a life worthy of the Lord and may please him in every way: bearing fruit in every good work, growing in the knowledge of God.

COLOSSIANS 1:10

59

WHOM DOES HE LOOK LIKE?

When each of my three sons was born, I just assumed they would look like me. I know that sounds a bit, well, arrogant, but it wasn't that at all. The simple fact was that I looked exactly like my dad—who looked like his dad. It would just make sense that my boys would look like me, right? While taking this for granted, I missed out on a great lesson about God's grandest desire for me—that I would put on the very characteristics of Christ himself, that I would "look" like Christ. It was in listening to the story of a friend that I learned this truth in an amazing way:

> The birth of each of my three children is burned in my brain in a way I can't exactly describe. It is the birth of my second child, first daughter, Alyx, however, that still sends shivers through my spine even though many years have passed. You see this child looked like me. For the first time ever in my life, I was looking at someone who shared many of my characteristics.
>
> Growing up, I was blessed by a mom and a brother who not only looked alike but who also shared many personality traits. I can remember, at times, wondering where in the world I came from—I was so different. I understand now that this is the magic of the mixing of the gene pool. While God creates each of us in a unique and special way, the genes of our family tree are usually evident somewhere.

When my first child, a son, was born, he looked exactly like his dad, who looked like his dad, who looked like his dad. None of these men seemed the least bit surprised that this brand-new addition resembled them. I yearned to see some part of me in this beautiful little angel, but alas, no, he was every bit his father's child. I even remember one day a friend of the family seeing me while visiting the small town in which my in-laws lived. He said, "I don't know who you are, but that baby has to be a"—and he went on to name my husband's family. Imagine that!

It is no wonder, then, that when I became pregnant for the second time, I thought every once in a while about what this baby might look like. She was not only the first girl in a line of men that counted back four generations, but she looked like her mother. I saw it in her eyes as soon as they were opened, but it was her tiny little hands that really took my breath away. They were an exact replica of mine. Every detail, except her fingerprints of course, was identical to mine. I was in awe of how God could do this. I had seen it before with others, like my son and the line of men before him, but to see this little person look so much like me was almost surreal. Isn't God amazing?

As my children have grown, I have seen that they really are a very unique blend of their ancestors before them. One has the ears of my uncle. Another has her grandmother's chin. Of course, one has my hands—that I've learned came from my father whom I never knew. Interestingly, their personalities are a true blend of their father and me. It seems like God took the best of both of us and planted these characteristics inside each of them. What amazing little miracles they are.

Just as God allows each of my children's genes to result in their physical features favoring their dad, me, or both, so God placed within each of our hearts spiritual genes that, if tendered correctly, will allow us to look more like Christ. This is, after all, God's desire—that when people see us, they will say that we look like Jesus. The more we seek his face, the more we love him, the more we will look like Christ. An amazing little miracle indeed.

Jesus grew in wisdom and stature, and in favor with God and men.

LUKE 2:52

166

YOU'RE AN EAGLE

I can relate to the story of the ugly duckling. The poor little duck wasn't really a duck at all. He had been born a swan, but he thought he was a duck. He was teased mercilessly by all the other ducks because he didn't look like them, he didn't quack like them, he didn't waddle like them. The bottom line: He was very different. The other ducklings kept quacking away, "Get out of here. Go away." If only they could have seen the end of the story!

Have you ever felt like an ugly duckling? Maybe you thought your nose was too big, or worse, maybe someone else told you that your nose was too big. Maybe it was the classroom that made you feel like the ugly duckling because you just didn't know the answers when the teacher called on you. You never felt as bright as that one kid who was right before you in the alphabetical order of tenth grade. Whether it's a smarter brain, smaller hips, longer legs, shorter feet, or a head that isn't quite so oval, we all have those moments of wishing we were built differently. The culture is filled with folks ready to take care of our issues with diet centers, fancy clothing boutiques, or the new anti-aging miracle centers lining local shopping malls. We are often willing to pay boatloads if we could just rid ourselves of the ugly duckling complex.

When I was a teenager, I felt like a bit of an ugly duckling because of my physical stature. Perhaps you're wondering, well how tall are you, Johnny? I am five feet eight inches tall. As a teenager I hated being called "little man." I know I wasn't called this in a belittling way (no pun intended), but it sounded derogatory, as if I did not measure up (pun intended). It hurts to play basketball and to always be the last one chosen—especially in those tender teen years. I used to think that maybe I should give up basketball and become a jockey. Horse racing was a sport that made heroes out of "little men."

A friend—and I use that word loosely—told me during college that my height would limit my success in life because people are automatically drawn to men over six feet tall. His idea of perfect was, well, about his size—six feet two inches and 190 pounds!

I remember when I was in my twenties, thinking, "I'm never going to date anyone taller than I am. Maybe I can find a gal that's just my height." This is a bit limiting in the world of dating, but the height issue seemed crucial to me at the time. I remember the list of questions that danced through my mind: How do you kiss a tall woman? How does a woman feel safe with a guy who's shorter than she is? Won't she feel like she's protecting me? As you can probably tell, this whole thing got a little ridiculous.

I wonder if David had some of these feelings when the prophet Samuel came to Jesse's house in search of the next king of Israel. Jesse was the father of seven sons, and he paraded them each before Samuel—excluding just one. He started with his oldest son, whom he considered to be most kinglike—capable, competent, the right height, with just the right bass in his voice, and the right moustache and beard. When Samuel rejected this son, Jesse brought out the next one. As he went through the boys in descending order of their ages, Samuel rejected them one after the other. "Surely you have one more," he said to Jesse, but Jesse protested. Remember that David was not included by Jesse. Why? Because David was an ugly duckling in his father's eyes—he wasn't the right height. Maybe Jesse and my college friend were roommates at some point!

Jesse replied to Samuel, "Surely you're not thinking of my son, David? He's a nobody, known only for playing with the sheep in the field. He's small, ruddy, skinny, he doesn't run very fast, and he can't jump very high. Well, okay, here he is, but I'm sure when you get a good look at him, you'll say no, he's definitely not the one." Jesse's protestations could not have been further from the truth.

When Jesse brought David out, the prophet Samuel took one look at David and almost immediately saw something that Daddy didn't. Of course, we all know the amazing path David's life took, and we also know that ugly duckling or not, he was a man to be used mightily by God.

You see, man may look at our outward appearance, but God looks only at our heart. When God looks at you and me, he doesn't see our weight or our height. He is not focused on how smart or not-so-smart we might be. He doesn't grade us based on our competence or lack thereof. He merely looks at the condition of our heart.

God helped me to really see that I wasn't an ugly duckling. He took me to Psalm 139:13–16, "For you created my inmost being; you knit me together in my mother's womb. I praise you because I am fearfully and wonderfully made; your works are wonderful, I know that full well. My frame was not hidden from you when I was made in the secret place. When I was woven together in the depths of the earth, your eyes saw my unformed body. All the days ordained for me were written in your book before one of them came to be." God made this message very clear to me, but I still really wrestled with the whole physical appearance thing twenty years ago. It was almost as if I heard God saying, "Johnny Parker, you were not in heaven when I was giving out looks and size and height. I really didn't ask your opinion. I didn't say, okay, Johnny, you're next. What color would you like to be, what style hair, what color eyes, how tall? You just name it and I'll make it so!" If God had given me that choice when I was twenty years old, I would have chosen to be a completely different me. I would have said, "No problem,

God, why don't we make it six foot three with a build like Arnold Schwarzenegger."

Well, it's been twenty years now, and at forty I've come to fully accept who I am, size and all. I'm still vertically challenged, but to be honest, I've been able to count it a blessing. Sure, there are times when the enemy tries to distract me. I'll hear conversations bounce through my head that say, "You know, that guy wouldn't have challenged you if you were taller," or "He would never have talked to you that way if you were more muscular." But then I'll step foot on a plane, sit down in my seat next to a long-legged man who can barely fit in the aisle, and find myself giving thanks for my tight, compact body!

God's love is not based on skin color, height, weight, bald, or beautiful. He is a lover of souls. He wants you to give your heart over to him so that you can soar like an eagle. He wants you to walk in newness of life each and every day, living your life with a destiny and purpose to which he has called you. Most importantly, he wants you to know that he loves you, and that is what matters most.

You were not created to be an ugly duckling; I was not created to be an ugly duckling; no one in God's perfect plan was ever created to be an ugly duckling. No matter what the world has said to you or what your mother and your father have said to you, you are fearfully and wonderfully made. God made you. God loves you. In him you are secure. Neither height, nor depth, nor weight, nor looks will ever be able to separate you from his love. Soar, baby, soar for God's glory.

I praise you because I am fearfully and wonderfully made.

PSALM 139:14

MAKING IT HOME
BEFORE THE DOOR
IS LOCKED

Did you have a curfew when you were a teen? Oh, how I remember those days. I went through a period of being pretty angry about the whole curfew thing—it just seemed so unfair. Of course, what a few years of parenting won't change! I know now that there's nothing unfair about teen curfews. It's actually the exact opposite. My parents weren't being uncaring or insensitive—they made the boundaries and expectations very clear because they loved me in a way I couldn't possibly know in my youth.

I was talking about the whole idea of a curfew the other day with a buddy of mine. His own curfew stories gave us both a good laugh. His dad expected him home at a certain time, and at exactly that time, the door was locked. His dad went to bed with absolutely no thought of getting up again. "Dad said, 'Once the lock goes on the door, that's it. Done for the night!'"

I thought about that, and I realized that in many ways that's what God has said to us. Second Corinthians 6:2 says: "I tell you, now is the time of God's favor, now is the day of salvation." The word *day* could be synonymous with the word *time*. So the verse would read, "Now is the time of salvation." We have this time period in which we are living, and we have the freedom to make the choice to receive Jesus or to reject Jesus. It's not God's will that any should perish. God's great hope is that we would all come to repentance because he, like curfew-enforcing fathers, loves us. He wants us to choose to make it home before it's too late. "Home" is our choosing to have a relationship with Jesus Christ, to fully experience him and his great love for us.

The problem is that many of us think the time for choosing Jesus is without bounds, but there is going to come a time when the door will close and be locked—tightly.

Matthew 25:1–13 tells this story in its entirety:

> At that time the kingdom of heaven will be like ten virgins who took their lamps and went out to meet the bridegroom. Five of them were foolish and five were wise. The foolish ones took their lamps but did not take any oil with them. The wise, however, took oil in jars along with their lamps. The bridegroom was a long time in coming, and they all became drowsy and fell asleep.
>
> At midnight the cry rang out: "Here's the bridegroom! Come out to meet him!"
>
> Then all the virgins woke up and trimmed their lamps. The foolish ones said to the wise, "Give us some of your oil; our lamps are going out."
>
> "No," they replied, "there may not be enough for both us and you. Instead, go to those who sell oil and buy some for yourselves."
>
> But while they were on their way to buy the oil, the bridegroom arrived. The virgins who were ready went in with him to the wedding banquet. And the door was shut.
>
> Later the others also came. "Sir! Sir!" they said. "Open the door for us!"
>
> But he replied, "I tell you the truth, I don't know you."
>
> Therefore keep watch, because you do not know the day or the hour.

You may be asking yourself, "Why does this matter? Why is it important for me to have a relationship with Jesus Christ?" Because Paul says, "God our Savior . . . wants all men to be saved and to come to a knowledge of the truth. For there is one God and one mediator between God and men, the man Christ Jesus, who gave himself as a ransom for all men" (1 Tim. 2:3–6). God wants you to be home with him—and the only way is through a relationship with Jesus Christ.

How about you? Where do you stand? Have you made it home? Are you in a relationship with Jesus Christ? A relationship with Jesus Christ involves acknowledging that you are a sinner, that I am a sinner, that we are all sinners. If you are ready to do that, then it's time to pray a prayer that goes something like this:

Dear Lord, forgive me; I am a sinner, and I have sinned against you. I believe that Jesus Christ died for me, and I place my faith in him and him alone. I ask that Jesus would come into my life, cleanse my life, forgive me of my sins, and make me the person he desires for me to be.

If you've prayed that prayer, then welcome home. Welcome home. Again, it's God's desire that we all make it home before it's too dark, before the lock goes on the door. The time is now. Make the choice, and take great comfort and peace in knowing that once you're home with God, you're home for good.

This is how much God loved the world: He gave his Son, his one and only Son. And this is why: so that no one need be destroyed; by believing in him, anyone can have a whole and lasting life. God didn't go to all the trouble of sending his son merely to point an accusing finger, telling the world how bad it was. He came to help, to put the world right again.

JOHN 3:16–17 MESSAGE

Johnny Parker is a pastoral counselor and speaks nationally for Family Life Marriage Conferences. He is a respected and sought after conference speaker nationally and internationally. He is the director of the Relationship Fitness Group, which exists to help singles, married couples, and professionals build strong relationships. Parker has been interviewed on CNN and BET. He and his family reside in Beltsville, Maryland.